OSPREY
MILITARY

CAMPAIGN SERIES     13

# HASTINGS 1066

GENERAL EDITOR DAVID G. CHANDLER

OSPREY MILITARY

# CAMPAIGN SERIES

13

# HASTINGS 1066

## THE FALL OF SAXON ENGLAND

### CHRISTOPHER GRAVETT

◄ *A Norman commander is identified by his rough club or 'baculum', a tradition that echoes the vine staff of the Roman centurion. It is also easier to see in battle as it is not properly fashioned mace. He wears mail leggings tied at the rear. The partially shaven head is typical of the current Norman fashion. (G. A. Embleton)*

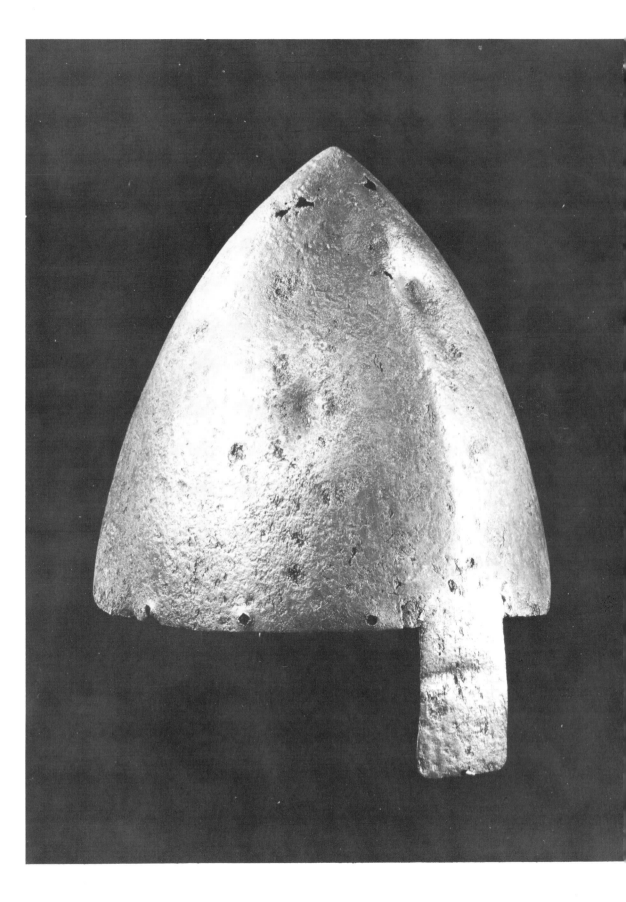

# CONTENTS

◄ *A conical helmet which was found near Olmütz in Moravia, similar in style to those depicted on the Bayeux Tapestry. This example is fashioned from a single piece of iron and the nasal or nose guard is integral with the helmet. The holes round the rim probably secured a leather strap internally, to which would have been sewn a padded lining. (Hof-jagd und rustkammer-sammlung, Vienna)*

First published in Great Britain in 1992 by Osprey, an imprint of Reed Consumer Books Limited, Michelin House, 81 Fulham Road, London SW3 6RB and Auckland, Melbourne, Singapore and Toronto

© 1992 Reed International Books Limited

Reprinted 1993, 1994 (twice)

*British Library Cataloguing in Publication Data*
Gravett, Christopher
Hastings 1066.
I. Title
942.021
ISBN 1-85532-164-5

Produced by DAG Publications Ltd for Osprey Publishing Ltd. Colour bird's eye view illustrations by Cilla Eurich. Cartography by Micromap. *Wargaming Hastings* by Andy Callan. Wargames consultant Duncan Macfarlane. Typeset by Ronset Typesetters, Darwen, Lancashire. Mono camerawork by M&E Reproductions, North Fambridge, Essex. Printed and bound in Hong Kong.

For a catalogue of all books published by Osprey Military please write to:

The Marketing Manager, Consumer Catalogue Department, Osprey Publishing Ltd, Michelin House, 81 Fulham Road, London SW3 6RB

**Acknowledgements:** I should like to thank Ian Eaves, Jeremy Hall, Thom Richardson and Karen Watts for their help and advice during the writing of this book.

For Jane, who has also been forced to suffer the Norman Conquest.

Lands of William of Normandy, under Direct Rule

Lands of William of Normandy, dependencies

0    50    100 Miles

0  50  100  150 Km

Northern Europe, at the time of the death of Edward the Confessor, 1066. England was divided into great earldoms, with the House of Leofric in the midlands and north, and the House of Godwin holding the south. Gyrth also controlled Oxfordshire. Siward of Northumbria's son, Waltheof, had recently been given his own earldom. William of Normandy's neighbours posed no threat to the Duke at this time.

# THE BACKGROUND TO THE CRISIS OF 1066

The year 1066 is perhaps the most famous date in English history. For contemporaries, however, the new year heralded an uncertain future. The old king, Edward, known as the Confessor, lay dying and had no children to succeed him. Matters were made more serious by the fact that Edward was predisposed towards the Norman duchy across the English Channel, and was likely to leave his kingdom to William of Normandy.

England contained a mixed population. The Romano-Celts had been overlaid gradually with Germanic Anglo-Saxon tribes who themselves subsequently faced pressure from the Viking threat in the 9th and 10th centuries. The Celts were now most numerous in Wales and Scotland. Scandinavians, largely Danish in origin, had settled in an area east of a line running roughly from the Wash to the Mersey that came to be known as the Danelaw. The Normans were also descendants of Viking adventurers who, under their leader Rollo, had settled in northern France in the 10th century.

Edward the Confessor was the son of King Ethelred II, later nicknamed 'Unraed', a term meaning 'No council' or 'Bad council' and subsequently corrupted to 'Unready'. Under pressure from fresh Danish attacks Edward and his brother Alfred were sent to the safety of the Norman court. Ethelred's second wife, Emma, was the sister of Duke Richard, an alliance that was useful in preventing Viking ships using Norman ports. Edward grew up in the duchy while his half-brother, Edmund 'Ironside', ruled briefly, to be followed by the Danish Cnut, then his sons Harold I and Harthacnut. On the latter's death in 1042 Edward was offered the crown.

The new king, having spent his formative years in Normandy, was uncomfortable in his new role. Moreover, he was surrounded by powerful earls. Leofric ruled the midland earldom of Mercia and Siward the vast stretches of Northumbria that encompassed most of England north of the Humber. Godwin, Earl of Wessex, was the head of a family that controlled all southern England. Edward always blamed him for the death of Alfred, blinded while in Godwin's charge on returning from Normandy in 1036. Edward was also married to Godwin's daughter, Edith, the earl obviously hoping for a grandson who would be a king. Furthermore, Godwin had a virtual alliance with the Count of Flanders.

Matters came to a head in 1051. Count Eustace of Boulogne, who was married to the King's sister, visited England and complained to Edward of the treatment he had received at Dover, where his men had fought with those holding the fortified enclosure or 'burh' Godwin was ordered to ravage the town but refused on the grounds that he would not attack part of his own earldom. He and his sons went into revolt, the northern earls sided with Edward, and England stood on the brink of civil war. Edward and his allies were able to banish the Godwins and send the queen to a nunnery.

It is extremely likely that the real reason for the unrest was Edward's persistent favour towards Normans and the question mark that lay over the succession. Edward had no heir and one rumour suggested that he was celibate. Two Norman chroniclers, the contemporaries William of Jumièges (writing *c.*1070-1) and William of Poitiers (writing *c.*1073-4), both assert that at this time Edward offered the throne to his cousin, William, word of which was carried to him by the Norman Archbishop of Canterbury. It could well be that Eustace was thus bringing the Ducal acceptance. He may also have been instructed to take the burh at Dover; this together with the lands of the See of Canterbury would provide a link to the Channel while cutting off Godwin from Flanders. The 'D' version of the contemporary *The*

VBI:NVNTII:VV

*Anglo-Saxon Chronicle* (probably compiled soon after the Conquest) and John of Worcester (writing *c.*1124-40) remark that in 1051 Duke William himself visited England. The motive may have been to pay homage to Edward. Certainly at this time the French king, alarmed at the prospect of a Norman duke possessed of England's wealth, abandoned his alliance with Normandy and opened negotiations with Anjou.

The Godwins forced their way back in 1052 and many Norman favourites fled. Godwin died the following year but his sons kept their stranglehold on the south. The eldest, Swein, was dead

▲ *Sent on an embassy to William probably in 1064, Earl Harold was seized on landing by Count Guy of Ponthieu. Here, William's messengers order Guy to bring his captive to the duke. The count appears to be wearing a sleeveless coat of scale armour. Such scales, probably of leather, bronze or iron, would have been attached to an undergarment and overlapped downwards.*

and Harold became Earl of Wessex. On the death of Siward in 1055 Northumbria was given to Godwin's third son, Tostig, whom Edward liked. In 1057 Gyrth, the fourth son, took over East Anglia together with Oxfordshire while his brother, Leofwine, was given an earldom that lay north of London in the Home Counties, as well as Kent. Aelfgar, who had vacated East Anglia to take over Mercia, died in 1062 and was succeeded by his son, Edwin. His other son, Morcar, obtained Northumbria three years later when the unpopular Tostig was expelled in a revolt. Thus the south lay in the hands of the Godwins and the north in those of Aelfgar's sons.

In 1054 the aetheling, Edward, son of Edmund Ironside and in exile ever since Cnut seized power, returned from Hungary. It is possible that the Confessor feared that his Norman policy would fail and felt that he could choose another candidate, since William had not actually been bestowed with the kingdom. However, with most of the pro-Norman magnates now gone, it seems likely that Harold wanted the aetheling to be designated heir so that there would be an English puppet on the throne. But no sooner had the aetheling reached England in 1057 than he mysteriously died.

Edward apparently maintained his support for William. Probably in 1064 or 1065 Harold went on a mission to Normandy, as can be seen on the Bayeux Tapestry, the famous embroidery almost certainly completed before 1083. If the year were 1065 Harold's power had probably been weakened and Edward could seize his chance to send him to confirm the offer of the throne for William. The earl's brother, Tostig, had been removed and, because Harold refused to help, he probably alienated his sister, the Queen. Even at this juncture Harold, lacking royal blood, may not have contemplated the throne but would have been eager to improve relations with William and secure his position as the prime magnate when the Duke became king. One excuse given by the English Eadmer (writing *c.*1095-1123) was that Harold wished to visit his younger brother and nephew, hostages since Godwin's revolt of 1051. The Earl landed on the opposite coast too far east and was promptly captured by Guy, Count of Ponthieu. One of the Englishmen managed to reach the Norman court and William ordered Harold's release, the two men meeting on the road.

It would appear from the accounts of Poitiers and Jumièges that Harold swore an oath of fealty

▼ *According to the Tapestry, Harold's oath to help William secure the English throne was taken at Bayeux. William of Poitiers locates it at Bonneville-sur-Touques, Orderic at Rouen. The Tapestry depicts the scene in the open air and shows* *two reliquaries, one portable, the other probably surmounted by a bull's eye as mentioned in 12th-century sources. Wace asserts that the relics were hidden. The Tapestry would hardly depict such a trick, even if true.*

VBI hAROLD:SACRAMENTVM:FECIT:~ hIC hAROL:D:D
VVILLELMO DVCI:~

and homage, becoming William's vassal and swearing to assist him to the throne. The story that holy relics were covered over to trick the earl does not appear until the account of Master Vace (writing *c.*1150-75), a chronicler who must be used with care. After the ceremony, William took Harold on campaign to Brittany (the Tapestry shows this before the oath) and finally sent him home laden with gifts and with one of the hostages. Harold had cultivated ties with several foreign princes and in any case could not be held indefinitely.

Edward died on 5 January 1066. The Tapestry shows his funeral in his newly consecrated church at Westminster on Friday the 6th. That same day was held the coronation of Harold. The contemporary *Vita Edwardi Regis* (probably written *c.*1065-7) describes the bequest. It attacks Archbishop Stigand, who was present and reports him as saying that the King was old and rambling, perhaps implying subversion at the scene. It also says that the kingdom was 'commended' to Harold. In the

▶ *During his stay in Normandy, Harold joined William on an expedition to demonstrate Norman power to the Bretons, among whom anti-Norman feeling had been stirred up. Several soldiers came to grief at the River Cuesnon and Harold here displays his bravery by rescuing two of them himself. Notice that the foot-soldiers wear no armour. Either they are light-armed, or else it was carried on supply wagons.*

*The keys of Dinan in Brittany are transferred by lance as token of surrender to the Normans. This is likely to be a simple representation of a motte rather than specifically that at Dinan, any trace of which has yet to be found. However, it shows the timber tower within a palisade which the Normans attempt to burn with torches. A flying bridge leads down to a ditch with counterscarp but the bailey is here omitted.* ▶

◀ *After the Breton campaign William bestowed arms on Harold in what is often taken to be a representation of the act of knighting, but may in fact be the creation of Harold as the Duke's vassal; the giving of a banner is significant. Notice Harold's sword which is worn beneath his mail. The square on the chest of some Norman hauberks probably represents a hanging ventail, a flap of mail which could be drawn up over the throat and chin, though it is also possible that it is a reinforce for the chest or a flap to cover the neck opening.*

same way, versions 'C' and 'D' of the *Chronicle* use the word 'entrusted', as though perhaps Harold was to hold it for William. The Anglo-Norman William of Malmesbury (writing *c.*1125) suggests that the bequest was had by force. In the Godwinist 'E' version of the *Chronicle*, John of Worcester and Eadmer maintain that Edward finally chose Harold, and even William of Poitiers seems to hint that this was the case, though he makes William say that it went against every action of Edward in the past. However, even if Harold were chosen by Edward and accepted by the nobles as the strongest and therefore the best candidate, the Normans did not accept the validity of last-minute changes of mind; in their eyes, the earlier bequest was binding. Moreover, Harold had broken his oath to William and the fateful events of 1066 were set in motion.

William was not the only candidate for the throne. There is a 13th-century story that Harthacnut had made a treaty with Magnus of Norway that if either died childless the other would inherit but that Magnus was prevented by his struggles with the Danes. *The Anglo-Saxon Chronicle* suggests rather that his son, the renowned fighter Harald Hardrada ('Hard Council'), was simply an opportunist awaiting his chance to invade England. The Danish king, Swein Estrithson, was so threatened by Norway that herein lies his reason for not pushing his own claim, as nephew of Cnut and grandson of Swein 'Forkbeard', but of offering support to William instead.

A further claimant was Edgar Aetheling, the son of the deceased aetheling from Hungary and grandson of Edmund Ironside. Although his claim was strong through kinship he was largely ignored because he was only about twelve years old. It is possible also that any succession claims for Edmund's heirs had been blocked by his father's second wife, Emma, in order to secure the throne for her sons Edward or Alfred. Edgar survived the upheavals to live quietly in the country.

Harold then had good reason to be troubled. After his coronation he rode north (for the first time in his life, by all accounts) to try to secure the support of Edwin and Morcar and the fickle northerners, who remembered the King as brother of the unattractive Tostig. Harold set aside his common-law wife, Edith Swan-Neck, and married her namesake, the sister of Edwin and Morcar, in an attempt to bind the two families together. He knew that he was threatened from both Normandy and Norway, and that an invasion could come either from the south or from the north. The problem lay in knowing which would materialize first.

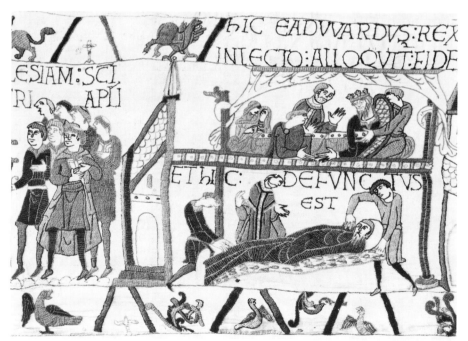

◀ *The death of Edward the Confessor, as depicted on the Bayeux Tapestry. The king's last moments are shown at the top. Queen Edith sits at his feet; her brother, Earl Harold, stands beside the bed. The tonsured priest is probably Stigand, the uncanonical Archbishop of Canterbury. Below, the body is wrapped for burial. These scenes follow those of the funeral and are deliberately misplaced so that the bequest is immediately followed by the coronation of Harold.*

# THE COMMANDERS

## William, Duke of Normandy

The illegitimate son of Duke Robert the Magnificent and Herleve, a tanner's daughter, William was born at Falaise in about 1028. He was soon plunged into the violent world of Norman politics when the magnates were ordered to swear fealty to the boy so that his father could set off on pilgrimage. When Robert subsequently died in 1035 the duchy fell into uproar and William, the new duke, barely escaped from assassins on several occasions. He grew up fully aware that survival depended on a close-knit following and the tactful handling of his lords. He knew that the Normans respected a strong-willed leader. About 5 feet 8 inches tall, and well-built, William wore his hair in the then-current Norman fashion, with the back and sides shaven. His bravery was not in question; he was ready to take the field in person and in his first battle at Val-ès-Dunes in 1047 he won praise for his valour, assisting his overlord the French king in securing a victory against Norman rebels.

Battles were exceedingly risky affairs, however. A victory did not always bring great rewards. Conversely, a mistake could mean a defeat, the duchy could be lost and the Duke might be killed. William was fully aware of this and followed the principles of contemporary warfare. Understanding the importance of the feudal castle he besieged strongholds to wear down his enemies with minimal risk. He realized the value of reconnaissance, personally taking part while before the Angevin-held Domfront in 1051 and also after landing at Pevensey. Here we are told he shouldered both his own hauberk and that of his exhausted companion, William fitzOsbern, a demonstration of his physical strength. However, the Duke also had a ruthless streak. When scouting from Domfront led to a night attack on Alençon, those defenders who insulted him by

*The castle of Falaise in Normandy. William was in all probability born here, perhaps in September 1028, though details come from 12th-century sources. The story that his father, Duke Robert, spied a local girl dancing is first encountered in William of Malmesbury. Her name (Herleve) is supplied by Orderic and birth place by Wace. The present rectangular keep was put up by the Conqueror's son, Henry I. (Courtesy of the French Government Tourist Office)*

beating hides in reference to his base birth were brutally mutilated; the town submitted, followed swiftly by Domfront. William learned that a short sharp show of violence could bring results.

Further external threats were also indirectly opposed. In two joint French and Angevin invasions of Normandy William refused battle but held his troops in the vicinity, waiting to pounce. At Mortemer in 1054 one half of the divided invading force scattered to plunder and was attacked by Robert of Eu. Three years later the rearguard of the invaders, having been separated from the army by the tide of the River Dives at Varaville, was set upon and cut to pieces. Thus it was that during the invasion of England William was actively seeking a battle to prevent his army from being outnumbered or bottled up and starved into submission. This would be only the second battle in which he was involved and the first in which he was in overall command.

## Harold II of England

In 1066 Harold was about 45 years old, the second son of Godwin, the Englishman who rose in the service of Cnut to become Earl of Wessex. Harold's mother was Gytha, Cnut's sister, and explains why the first four male children of Godwin bore Scandinavian names. The Bayeux Tapestry suggests that Harold wore a moustache in what appears to have been a fashion of the day in England. He entered the Earldom of Wessex on his father's death in 1053.

Evidence of Harold's military skills before 1066 comes largely from his expeditions against King Gruffydd of North Wales and his ally, Aelfgar of Mercia. When Hereford was sacked in 1055 Earl Harold arrived with the English army and camped on the Welsh side of the border while a fortified burh was constructed around the town. In order to improve the defences he appointed burghers as liable for military service. The mountainous terrain forced a settlement but further unrest followed. In a second revolt by Aelfgar, in which not only Gruffydd but also a Norse fleet was involved, the Mercian earl was again reinstated. Harold must have been aware that Aelfric would never live at ease with his southern rivals but he

restrained any impulses to remove the rebel; he may also have hoped to isolate Gruffydd. By contrast, against Gruffydd's persistent raiding Harold displayed the swift action that would be seen again in 1066. He completely surprised the Welsh by leading an assault force out of Gloucester in the midwinter of 1062, crossing the Dee and seizing the headquarters at Rhuddlan. As the campaigning season was over Gruffydd barely escaped capture. This was followed up by a two-pronged attack the following May in which Harold took a fleet from Bristol towards the Welsh coast while his brother Tostig launched a land-based attack from the north. Harold's reputation was known to the Welsh chronicler Giraldus who, writing in about 1193, notes how the Earl taught his men to mimic the Welsh by discarding their mail for lighter armour and by using javelins. He so intimidated his enemies that Gruffydd was killed by his own men for refusing to negotiate and his head was brought to Harold. The campaign had taken less than three months; the removal of this threat made Harold a respected and popular figure.

The dash and flair shown by Harold are typical of his temperament. It seems likely that this was known to William, perhaps through observation of the earl in the Breton campaign during his visit to Normandy probably in 1064. By contrast, Harold may have misjudged William as being too cautious after seeing how he withdrew from Dol when supplies were threatened and how he was content to come to terms after Conan allied with Geoffrey of Anjou. If so, it shows a fatal misunderstanding of William's strategy. A further defect may be contained in the remark of William of Malmesbury that a number of men refused to join Harold at Hastings because he would not share the spoils after the battle of Stamford Bridge, though he may have wished to retain the ships and equipment until the Norman threat had passed. Nevertheless Harold's reputation as a leader remains high. Unusually for the times, in 1066 three battles were fought at both ends of the country in less than a month. Harold fought in the latter two and only just lost the second. The King was ably supported at Hastings by his younger brothers, Gyrth and Leofwine.

# OPPOSING ARMIES

## The Army of Duke William

In Normandy the magnates, often members of the ducal family, were the chief source of troops. Much of the land in the duchy before 1066 was held by powerful lords as hereditary estates, knights being sent for service to the Duke as a duty, though there is little evidence for fixed quotas. Similar arrangements were made for some religious houses. At this time tenures were slowly changing into fiefs and, associated with these, grants of land from the duke for which homage and fealty were performed. It is possible that more precise numbers of knights were expected for feudal service. The length of service expected at this date was probably about 40 days a year. Many of these knights might live at their lord's hall at his expense as household knights, but others were settled on part of his estates on their own holdings. Wealthier knights in their turn might be expected to supply their lord with a number of troopers who either lived as household men or were given a parcel of land. Often lords had far more knights in their service than were required for the duke. A contingent of horsemen was formed into a 'conrois'; evidence suggests that this was organized by multiples of five into perhaps groups of 25 or 50. Knights might also be expected to bring their followers who served as infantry or less well-armed cavalry. For the expedition to England Wace insists that the Duke managed to extract promises from his magnates for twice the normal quota of men.

The military arrangements in the emerging feudal duchy were complex since magnates and tenants might be enfeoffed of each other, resulting in a man holding land of two lords who subsequently went to war. Moreover William never enjoyed in Normandy the sort of control he later maintained in England, where he was able to impose a new feudalization on the conquered country, one in which all land ultimately belonged to the king.

Knights rode expensive warhorses and required assistants to look after their equipment and serve them in the field. The evidence for squires at this date is shadowy. Certainly young men of free birth were recruited and trained in the school

▼ *French knights, here depicted as horsemen, riding beasts in the* Apocalypse of S. Sever, *produced between 1028 and 1072. The figures at the top appear to have helmets composed of riveted segments; those below may be fluted. All sleeves are wrist length, unusual at such an early date, though a few knights on the Bayeux Tapestry also may be wearing similar long sleeves. (Bibliothèque Nationale lat. 8878 fl48v)*

of mounted warfare, later evidence suggesting that they were not expected to wear full armour or to bear swords in battle until they had been knighted. There also seems to be a case for those of lower birth who were simply mounted servants and who attended the knight.

The left wing of William's army consisted of Bretons probably under Alan Fergant, cousin of the ruling count and serving as a nominal vassal of Normandy. His followers obviously expected lucrative gains in the conquered land. The feudal levy of Normandy was supplemented also by large numbers of mercenary horse and foot, especially from neighbouring areas of France and Flanders and even Poitou and Aquitaine, attracted by prospects of loot. The blessing of the pope gave the enterprise an aura of respectability.

A large number of infantrymen took part in the invasion. Some would have accompanied their lords as foot-soldiers, or have been summoned by the old 'arrière-ban'. Many others would be mercenaries serving the duke for pay. These would have included not only spearmen but a large number of archers and crossbowmen.

The main defensive garment worn over the tunic was the coat of mail, called a 'hauberk'. Mail consisted of hundreds of individually formed interlinked and riveted iron rings. Many coats were knee-length, the skirts split front and rear to facilitate riding, and provided with elbow-length sleeves. Some were extended to form a mail hood

▼ *This picture of the Norman attack on Dol in Brittany appears to portray light-armed horsemen with no body armour except for the leading figure who wears a helmet perhaps with neckguard and coif. Are the figures depicted here light cavalrymen, squires, who were not allowed to wear mail, or simply knights on the march who have rushed into action without donning full armour?*

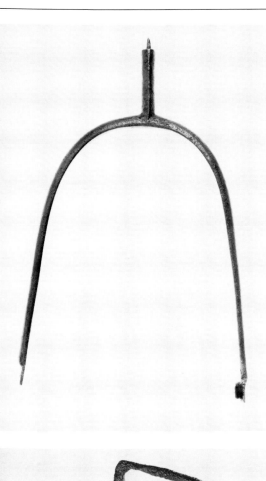

◀ *An 11th-century prick spur. Such spurs were usually of iron and riveted to stirrup leathers. Other versions as shown on the Bayeux Tapestry have small pyramidal or conical points. (Museum of London)*

▼ *This Norman depiction of David and Goliath from the late 11th-century St. Augustine's Commentaries portrays Goliath as wearing a hauberk with short, undivided skirts and a loose hood. He carries an older style circular shield. David gives a good impression of a Norman slinger, a number of whom may have been present in William's army. Unarmoured, his slingstones are carried in a shoulder bag. (Bib. Munic. Rouen, MS A 19)*

◀*An English stirrup derived from those used by the Vikings, with side bars which hang below the tread and which are sometimes decorated. Loop stirrups might also be seen, while the Normans additionally used a more triangular style. Stirrups served to hold a man in his saddle and were ideal for mounted warfare, a fact the Normans exploited well. With long leathers the horsemen rode almost standing in their stirrups. (Courtesy of the Board of Trustees, Royal Armouries)*

◄ A Norman knight and an unarmoured retainer from his household. The square depicted on the chest of some knights on the Bayeux Tapestry is here interpreted as a loosened ventail to guard the throat. Other figures, both Norman and English, show a single horizontal strap, which may be a laced ventail. The leather strapping on the forearms is suggested by the bands seen on some figures wearing mail coats, since nowhere on the Tapestry are civilian tunics given looped sleeves. Notice the sword worn beneath the armour. (Ed Dovey)

► A mail shirt from Verdal, North Tronderlag in Norway, of later date but similar to those of the 11th century. Each iron ring is interlinked with four others and closed by a rivet. Similar short coats might be worn by English and Norman warriors who did not possess the more recent longer style. Mail is very difficult to date and extremely rare from this period. A complete coat, associated with St. Venceslas and possibly of the 11th century, is to be found in Prague. (University Museum of National Antiquities, Oslo)

A few hauberks appear from pictorial evidence to have been made from scales of metal, horn or leather fastened to an undergarment. Hauberks of padded cloth may also have been used, or even a few of hide, though information is extremely scarce. Similar padded coats may have been worn beneath mail to absorb blows, as the metal links were flexible, but again the earliest evidence for such defences is from the 12th century. It is possible also that some wore a quilted or leather hood with their mail coat rather than one of mail attached to the hauberk. Some hauberks shown in illuminated manuscripts as reaching the hip or thigh may have been worn largely by foot-soldiers.

Some Normans, notably Duke William, are portrayed with mail sleeves that protrude from under the hauberk sleeve. Moreover, leggings of mail are shown occasionally. Ordinary leather shoes were worn, the horsemen wearing iron prick spurs terminating in small points.

The helmet was conical in shape, usually fitted with a nasal-guard and sometimes with reinforcing bands. An illustration on the Tapestry of Duke William shows what appear to be ties like those on

# ORDERS OF BATTLE
# THE NORMAN AND ENGLISH ARMIES

Relatively little hard evidence exists for the composition of the armies at Hastings. Few who came with Harold are named. Some individuals in the Norman army are known from contemporary sources, and a list of 32 persons has been compiled by Professor David Douglas. The Battle Abbey Roll only survives in copies, since it disappeared in the 14th century; it may have originally been a list taken at Dives. A 19th century list was inscribed on the wall of the church at Dives and another compiled in 1931 and enrolled on a tablet in the Château at Falaise. The list compiled by David Douglas includes:

Eustace, Count of Boulogne
Robert, Count of Mortain
William, son of Richard, Count of
  Evreux
Geoffrey, son of Rotrou, Count of
  Mortagne
Odo, Bishop of Bayeux
Geoffrey, Bishop of Coutances
William fitzOsbern
Aimeri, Vicomte of Thouars
Walter Giffard
Ralf of Tosny
Hugh of Montfort
Hugh of Grandmesnil
William of Warenne
Robert, son of Roger of Beaumont
William Malet
Gulbert of Auffay
Robert of Vitot
Engenulf of Laigle
Gerelmus of Panileuse
Robert fitzErneis
Roger, son of Turold
Turstin, son of Rollo (probably bore
  the papal banner)
Erchembald, son of Erchembald the
  Vicomte
Vitalis
Wadard
Taillefer

A member of the house of Ponthieu
  (possibly Count Guy I)
Gerald the Seneschal
Rodolph the Chamberlain (of
  Tancarville)
Hugh of Ivry, the Butler
Richard fitzGilbert
Pons

## THE NORMAN ARMY

As there are no firm figures for numbers present, any pronouncement must be highly speculative. If William's army is estimated to have consisted of 7,500 combatants and it is accepted that the Breton division was larger than the Franco-Flemish while that of the Normans was larger than the others combined, a tentative breakdown of the invading army at Hastings may be as follows:
**Franco-Flemish** under William fitzOzbern and Eustace of Boulogne: 1,500
(archers, 300; heavy infantry, 800; cavalry, 400)
**Normans** under Duke William: 4,000
(archers, 800; heavy infantry, 2,130; cavalry, 1,070)
**Bretons** probably under Alan Fergant: 2,000
(archers, 400; heavy infantry, 1,070; cavalry, 530)

### The Ship List of William the Conqueror
Possibly compiled after 13 December 1067 or c.1072

| | | Ships | Knights |
|---|---|---|---|
| 1. | William fitzOsbern | 60 | |
| 2. | Hugh of Avranches | 60 | |
| 3. | Hugh of Montfort | 50 | 60 |
| 4. | Remigius of Fécamp | 1 | 20 |
| 5. | Nicholas, Abbot of St. Ouen | 15 | 100 |
| 6. | Robert, Count of Eu | 60 | |
| 7. | Fulk d'Aunou | | 40 |
| 8. | Gerold the Seneschal | | 40 |
| 9. | William, Count of Evreux | | 80 |
| 10. | Roger of Montgomery | | 60 |
| 11. | Roger of Beaumont | 60 | |
| 12. | Odo, Bishop of Bayeux | 100 | |
| 13. | Robert, Count of Mortain | 120 | |
| 14. | Walter Giffard | 30 | 100 |

Total number: 776 ships

## THE ENGLISH ARMY
Few names are known of men who fought for Harold, nor how they were disposed in the line. His brothers, Gyrth and Leofwine, were probably in the front line with their bodyguards, perhaps to the right and left of the king's headquarters. Other probable combatants, mentioned in chronicles or in the Domesday Book, are:

Esegar, Sheriff of Middlesex
Leofric, Abbot of Peterborough
Aelfurg, Abbot of Winchester
Sheriff Godric, Lord of Fifhide
Thurkill of Kingston
Eadric the deacon

Numbers involved can only be supposition: King Harold II would have had a bodyguard of housecarls and king's thegns around the standard.

**English battle line:**
800 household troops (less bodyguard for King)
6,500 fyrd
700 fyrd militia
More fyrdmen, late for the battle, may
  have arrived during the day.

▲An antler fragment from Sigtuna, Uppland, shows a Viking warrior wearing a conical helmet fitted with a nasal to protect the nose. Such helmets were by far the commonest form used by Scandinavian fighting men as well as by their English and Norman counterparts. The vertical row of circles implies a helmet made in sections that were riveted together; those round the brim suggest rivets for an internal lining. (Antikvarisk-topografiska arkivet, Stockholm. Photograph: Sören Hallgren)

▲A conical helmet, traditionally that of St. Wenceslas and now in Prague Cathedral. Fashioned from a single piece of iron, it features a nasal integral with a browband the decoration on which possibly dates it to the 10th or 11th centuries.

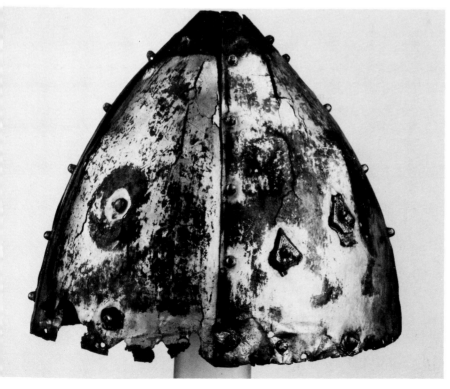

◄A conical helmet of East European origin but again similar to those on the Tapestry. This shows an alternative production technique; the helmet is made from four overlapping segments riveted together. Such seams occur on examples depicted on the Tapestry. Both types of helmet might also have had applied iron bands, which in the latter case would have covered the joints. The segments might have been painted; here the surface has been gilded. (Liverpool Museum, on loan to Royal Armouries)

a bishop's mitre hanging from the back of his helmet and which may be symbols of rank. Helmets were laced under the chin to prevent loss in battle.

Most warriors used a shield. Some infantrymen carried a circular wooden shield, often faced and perhaps backed with leather. An iron boss riveted to the centre of the surface covered a hole through which the hand grasped the shield by an iron strip riveted inside. Many probably had a second strap to secure the forearm, while a 'guige' strap allowed the shield to be slung on the back or hung up, as well as preventing it being lost if dropped. The edges may have been protected by applied bands of metal, leather or even painted wood. However, horsemen and many infantrymen now carried a kite-shaped shield with a rounded top, drawn out to a point at the bottom. It was said to be ideal for the horseman as the long shape protected the rider and could be held horizontally to protect the horse's flank. All the Normans in the Tapestry carry this type. The shield faces bear designs of dragons, lions or crosses of various form, though true heraldry had not developed at this date, a fact that is demonstrated by the way William is portrayed wearing several different devices on his shield. The 'enarmes' or holding straps took various forms, often a square of straps for forearm and hand (possibly framing a pad to cushion the arm against bruising from blows); there was also a 'guige' strap. Some bore a metal

boss riveted to the front but only serving as decoration.

The warrior's favourite weapon was the straight, double-edged slashing sword, which was highly esteemed. The other main weapon of the knight was the lance, a plain ash shaft about eight feet in length tipped with a socketed leaf-shaped or triangular iron head. It could be thrown like a javelin, used to stab overarm or tucked ('couched') under the right arm and levelled against the enemy, imparting the full force of horse and rider to the iron tip. When used in a concerted charge, the riders knee to knee, such a shock was extremely effective. Anna Comnena, the Byzantine princess who saw western knights at the time of the First Crusade, said that a charging knight could punch a hole in the walls of Babylon. However, the couched lance was relatively novel at this time; moreover at Hastings the terrain was unfavourable and the knights faced a solid phalanx of foot. The evidence suggests that in 1066 the knights charged in groups, each contingent following the 'gonfanon' or pennon on the lance of their feudal lord. Slim, socketed javelins and broader bladed stabbing spears were carried by the infantry.

Two other banners are worthy of mention. The first appears on the Tapestry on a half moon-shaped flag with flies, and depicts a raven (earlier thought to be a chalice and thus the holy papal banner). The raven banner was a Viking flag and

▼ *Spears were of two kinds: those for thrusting had broad, leaf or lozenge-shaped heads; javelins had long, slender heads. Both types were occasionally decorated with inlays of* brass or silver. The barbed heads shown on many manuscripts are rarely borne out in archaeological finds and are probably stylistic representations. (Museum of London)*

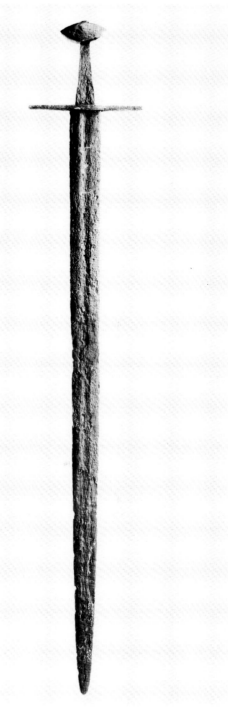

◀ *A French infantry formation of overlapping shields, from the Apocalypse of S. Sever of 1028-72. It demonstrates that the 'shield wall' was not confined to the Anglo-Saxons. Feudal societies in which knights predominated also made use of it. (Bibliothèque Nationale, MS lat.8878)*

▶ *The 'brazil-nut' pommel was a form which lasted from the early 11th to the late 12th centuries. Together with the 'tea-cosy' form it was probably the commonest type at the time of the Norman* Conquest, used by both English and French soldiers. Swords were sheathed in wooden scabbards which were often leather covered and lined with wool or fur to keep the blade naturally* oiled. A metal chape protected the tip and richer examples might have an ornamented metal mouthpiece or locket. (By kind permission of James Pickthorn, Esq.)*

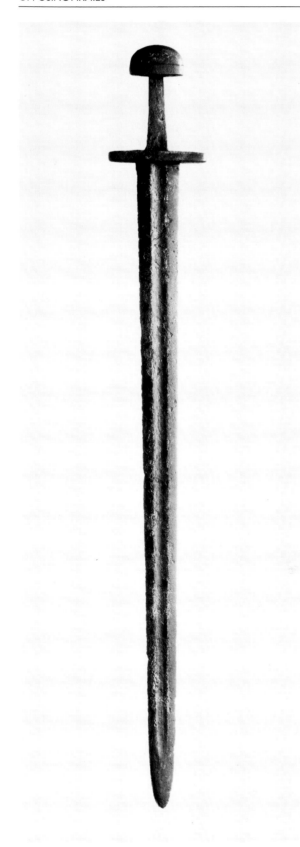

*◄Some swords were pattern welded. Several metal bars, each consisting of twisted rods of iron and mild steel, were forged together in a sort of sandwich, and the resultant pattern on the ground blade gave the process its name. Edges of harder metal were added. By the 11th century many swords were being made from combinations of iron and better quality steel. The hardness of the latter also tended to make the blade brittle so a balance was necessary between the more malleable iron and the harder steel whereby a sword was sturdy but flexible. Many swords at this date bore a characteristic 'tea-cosy' pommel. (By kind permission of James Pickthorn, Esq.)*

was carried by Harald Hardrada, the other invader in 1066. It is a timely reminder that, despite their vigorous church policy, the Viking ancestry of the Normans was not far below the surface. Around Bayeux, 'Thor aid!' was the battle cry rather than 'Dex Aie!' ('God's Aid'). The other banner seen on the Tapestry is carried by Eustace of Boulogne and is white with a golden cross. The size of the flag, together with the device, strongly suggests that this is the papal banner granted to William. A gold cross on white became the papal arms which showed their special case by defying the rules of heraldry

Some knights may have carried a mace. Three types appear on the Tapestry. One seems to have a flanged iron head in the style of later maces. Others, carried by fleeing Englishmen, have knobbed heads rather like the metal heads of surviving 12th-century examples. These are small but capable of breaking bones even through flexible mail. The third type is carried by Duke William and Odo and is a rough 'baculum', a baton of command, making it easily distinguishable from the ordinary mace. In this respect it harks back to the vine rod of the Roman centurion.

Warhorses or 'destriers' were carefully bred and combined power and mobility. William himself was sent two black horses by the King of Spain, where prized animals were reared. The Tapestry highlights the fact that such mounts were full stallions.

The archers on the Tapestry are all unarmoured except for one figure in mail. It seems likely in the light of recent finds that the weapon in use was a wooden selfbow, usually about five

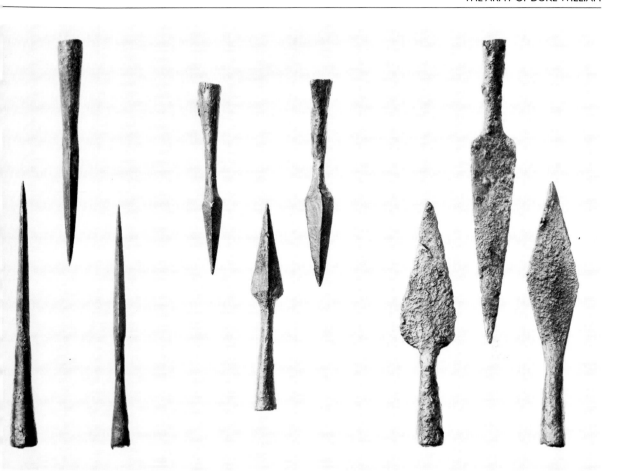

and a half to six feet in length. It may have differed from the longbow – whose power the Normans felt when they ventured into Wales in the next century – in having less draw weight or being drawn a shorter distance, perhaps to the chest. Effective range against a mailed opponent may have been 100 yards. One bowman shown on the Tapestry chasing Englishmen after the battle may be riding a captured horse, though his spurs suggest he might be a mounted archer who would have used a horse for transport.

Though none is shown on the Tapestry, William of Poitiers states that William also used crossbowmen. The square-headed bolts are specifically mentioned in the *Carmen de Hastingae Proelio*, which is thought to date from between 1067 and 1075, although some maintain that it is a 12th-century poem. In appearance crossbowmen would have looked very much like the archers except that each carried a crossbow with wooden bow and tiller. Probably slightly more powerful

*▲ Arrows found in largely late 11th or 12th-century levels at Bell Wharf, Southwark Bridge, in London. The three leaf-shaped heads contrast with the four-sided examples which were previously thought to be a later type. The latter heads would have been particularly effective in bursting mail rings apart. The effectiveness of archery in 1066 was probably surprisingly good. (By kind permission of Anthony de Reuck, Esq.)*

than the selfbow, the crossbow at this time could be loaded by bracing the bow against the feet and pulling back the cord by hand. Short wooden bolts with iron heads and parchment vanes were carried in belt quivers. Slingers may also have taken part. Unarmoured, these men carried a pouch holding slingshot with an effective range of about 30 yards. They could be lethal at close range; a blow to the unprotected face might kill or maim.

Medieval chroniclers are notoriously vague in their estimates of troops taking part in a battle. Even in a relatively well-documented conflict such

as Hastings, the calculation of numbers present is largely based on intelligent guesswork. One cannot accept chroniclers' wildly exaggerated figures for combatants, a fraction of whom could not possibly fit on the field, quite apart from the problems of supply so created. At Hastings attempts have been made to calculate the number in William's army by estimating the total of men each ship could carry. Wace is the only chronicler to give a reasonable figure of 696 ships and even this has been questioned, while many of the ships carried horses and provisions as well. Other considerations must be taken into account, such as the size of the field. The length of the English line on the ridge may offer some clue, although its depth cannot be known for certain. Luckily the battlefield has been located fairly precisely, since William built the high altar of his new abbey on the spot where Harold fell. The early church has been located on the ridge and, despite ground alterations to site the abbey buildings, the field itself can be traced approximately. There is also the likelihood that the two armies were not greatly dissimilar in size, the Normans having perhaps slightly fewer men. Such factors suggest a total invading force of about 10,000 men, which, when due account is taken of sailors, cooks, carpenters and other non-combatants, leaves a figure of about 7,500 soldiers. The Norman army can be divided tentatively into 2,000 horsemen, 4,000 heavy infantrymen and 1,500 archers and crossbowmen.

## The English Army

The Anglo-Danish forces employed by the English kings in the 11th century can be separated into the household troops and fyrd. Anglo-Saxon kings and great lords had always employed bodyguards who would surround them in battle and if necessary die for their master. In 1018 Cnut paid off his men but retained the crews of 40 ships, some 3,000 to 4,000 men, who were formed into a royal guard with richly decorated weapons and code of conduct. However, they appear to have had nothing to do with housecarls. It is often supposed that the lifestyle of these men was influenced by that of the legendary Jomsvikings, a pirate brotherhood with its own code of conduct, though the authority of such sagas is historically dubious. Moreover, much of the evidence for the housecarls and their organization in England comes from late 12th-century Scandinavian sources whose relevance for the 11th century has recently been questioned. If such a formidable standing army were available to Edward the Confessor, why was it not employed swiftly to crush the revolt of 1051? It seems likely that the housecarls were actually household troops and were comparable to the native thegns, well-trained fighters some of whom lived at the court or hall of the king or earls and received a wage. Some might be settled on their own estates, in which case the name 'housecarl' probably denoted their foreign origin. Those of sufficient status came to the host with their tenants. It is quite likely that such men had some code of discipline. Some were certainly living at Wallingford on the Thames, though there is no reason to suppose that, because this was a strategically important fording place, they also acted as garrison troops.

Together with the household troops were the men of the fyrd who performed military duties ('fyrdfaereld') as part of their service in return for the land they held of the king, together with fortress work ('burhbot') and bridge repairs ('brycegeweorc'). The Berkshire Custumal in *Domesday Book* shows that here one man was required from every five hides. The hide was a unit apparently assessed on the economic worth of land. It has been suggested that one man from every six carucates was the measure in the Danelaw. At this time the five-hide unit was the mark of a thegn, a man of substance. A ceorl or peasant might have a mail coat and gold sword but unless he held the required land he remained a ceorl. The thegn was probably expected to attend the muster armed with helmet and mail; four shillings from each hide were for provisions or pay. If no thegn were present a higher-ranking peasant was presumably

*Norman crossbowmen using primitive crossbows with wooden bow arms. The power required to hand-draw the weapon fixed the strength. A padded coat is worn by one man, though no certain representations are known at this date, unless the trellis or triangular patterns on some depictions of armour are so interpreted. (Rick Scollins)*

▲ *A manuscript illustration of c.1000 depicting an Anglo-Saxon warrior wearing a shirt apparently of mail or leather. A brooch or pin secures the cloak on the right shoulder to leave the arm free. Note the spirally wound 'puttees' on the leg and the puckered tunic sleeves, features common to English dress. (By permission of The British Library, MS Cotton Cleopatra C. viii f30)*

equipped by the other land-holders in the unit in proportion to their own holdings, though this remains speculative. King's thegns who owned large tracts of land and held rights of jurisdiction brought one man for each five hide unit possessed. Fyrdmen were expected to serve beyond their borders and even beyond the sea if required. The Worcester Custumal does not mention the five-hide unit and, being the only other source, it is uncertain whether the five-hide and six-carucate units were universal in England. According to the Worcester Custumal, the wealthy king's thegn lost his land if he failed to do service, because of his close relationship to the crown. If a lesser thegn (one probably commended to a king's thegn) brought another in his place he paid a 40 shilling fine to his lord. If nobody came the lord received 40 shillings but gave it to the king (50 shillings in the Berkshire Custumal). Towns were also assessed, being expected to supply up to twenty men depending on the number of hides held.

In time of war the fyrd could be called up for a period of two months. In an emergency this could be repeated; in 1016 such a summons occurred five times. The death penalty could be enforced for desertion when the king was present with his army; Cnut's laws proclaim loss of life and

◀ *A rare fragment of 11th-century English sculpture depicts the lower half of a mail-clad warrior. As in the Bayeux Tapestry, the mail looks like trousers. While it is just possible that split skirts were tied round the legs of infantrymen, it is more likely to be a conventional*

*way of showing divided skirts. The sword belt appears to have a supporting strap lower down the scabbard which is attached to the belt at rear and serves to hold the sword back at an angle. (Copyright Winchester Excavations Committee)*

▼*Although it is unlikely that the English fought on horseback, the wealthier members of the army certainly possessed horses and rode to the battlefield, their mounts then being tethered in rear. Although their saddles and stirrups were essentially similar to those of the Normans, the*

*value of cavalry in warfare was not appreciated. Conversely, after Hastings the Normans several times dismounted their knights to fight. (By permission of The British Library, MS Cotton Claudius Biv f25)*

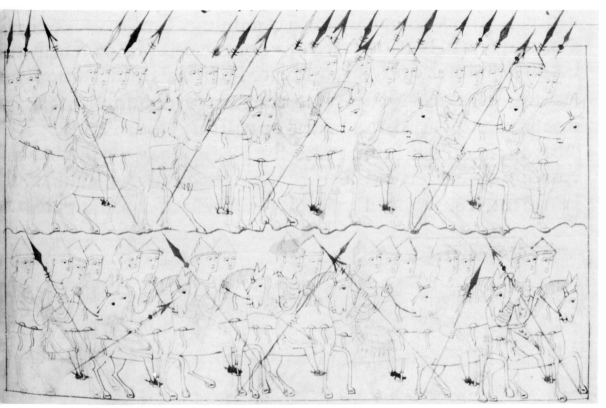

property for leaving one's lord. Conversely death in action at the lord's side meant that the latter would remit the 'heriot' (death duty) and allow the heirs to succeed to the dead warrior's estates. Evidence suggests that the fyrd was divided up into units based on the 'hundreds' (or districts) of each shire, which implies that a decimal system was in use. The king commanded the army, assisted by his immediate subordinates, the great earls. Beneath them were the housecarls and king's thegns with their retinues of commended lesser thegns or higher peasants.

In time of national emergency, as in 1066, the king could also call upon the services of every able-bodied freeman. The duty was confined to the shire boundaries and for a single day, otherwise the service was paid. For campaigns against the Welsh and Scots a 15-day period of service appears to have been more usual. This militia was of questionable value and was probably primarily used for garrisoning towns or for coastal defence. In some areas garrison duty in the communal burh was required; two sources indicate that an acre's breadth of wall should be maintained by sixteen hides, one man to a hide, though such duties replaced fyrd service.

Most housecarls and wealthier thegns rode to battle but dismounted and fought on foot. A good deal of ink has been spilt in recent years in trying to prove that the English army sometimes fought as cavalry and could have done so against the Normans if William had not marched out and forced Harold to take up a defensive position on the ridge at Battle. Since cavalrymen require much training in order to perfect the art of mounted combat, it is argued that the professional house-carls (considered before their status was reviewed) would be the most likely candidates. Evidence for the use of English cavalry is slender, to say the least. The most obvious pointer is the comment by the Icelandic chronicler, Snorri Sturluson, in his great work *Heimskringla*, that at the battle of Stamford Bridge Harold's men rode against the Norwegian line of shields. However, Snorri (writ-

ing *c.*1223-35) seems to have received garbled accounts of Norman tactics at Hastings that were then utilized in his account of Stamford Bridge. An example of what happened when the English did act as cavalry can be found in *The Anglo-Saxon Chronicle* under the year 1055. Earl Ralph, the

▼ *The Gjermundbu helmet is a rare survival from 10th-century Norway. It is fitted with a 'spectacle' guard cut from a sheet of iron. No such helmets appear in 11th-century sources but it is not impossible that one or* two similar specimens *may have been worn by leading Norse warriors during their attack on Yorkshire in 1066. (University Museum of National Antiquities, Oslo Photograph: L. Pedersen)*

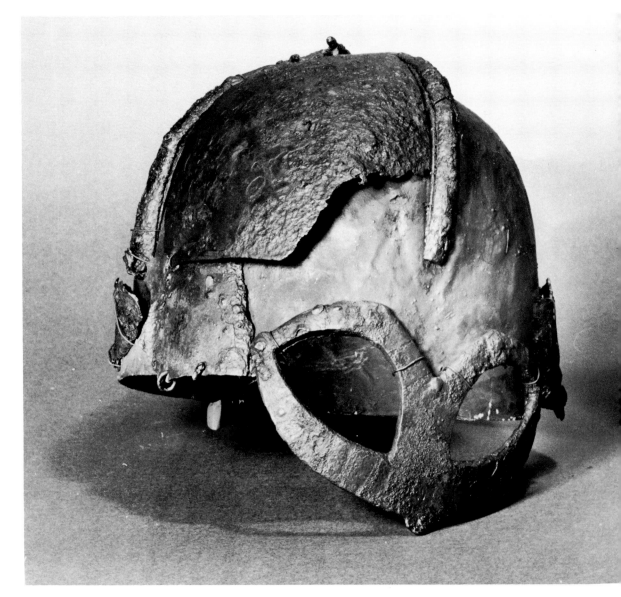

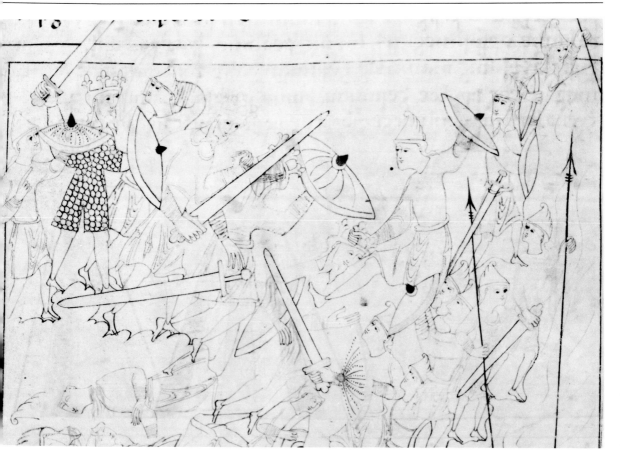

Norman nephew of King Edward, was routed by the Welsh in the rolling country around Hereford and 'the English fled, because they had been made to fight on horseback'.

The coastal towns of Kent and Sussex – Pevensey, Dungeness, Romney, Hythe, Folkestone and Sandwich – probably supplied housecarls or warriors for naval service together with ships, a system that would eventually form into the Cinque Ports organization. A national ship levy was also imposed whereby each 'ship-soke' (often of three hundreds) supplied a vessel. The fyrd service produced men for sea as well as land service, often 60 being so assigned. Sometimes this may have been commuted for a money payment or 'ship-scot'. Wealthier men might also provide ships with the condition that they be allowed their use when not needed.

In armour and weaponry the English army was similar in many respects to that of the Normans. The housecarls and thegns were equipped with comparable hauberks which they called 'byrnies'.

*▲ An English manuscript of c. 1020-50 showing a king dressed in a mail coat which has been added later and is very like those seen on the Bayeux Tapestry. His shield-bearer is one of those wearing Phrygian caps, most probably of leather. Swords display both the older lobated and early forms of disc pommel. The lugs on the spear sockets are probably mouldings. Such 'winged' spears existed with two lugs to guard against enemy weapons sliding down the shaft and to prevent deep penetration making withdrawal difficult, but they were a Carolingian style and rare by this date. (By permission of The British Library, MS Cotton Claudius B.iv f24v)*

The Tapestry shows both kite shields and round shields (a few of the latter possibly oval in shape) in the hands of Englishmen.

The main difference between English and Norman weaponry lay in the English use of the axe. On the Tapestry two kinds of fighting axe are shown. The first was the Danish axe, with a cutting edge of about four inches, mounted on a light haft, which could be swung with one hand. The most popular axe, however, was the broadaxe. This had

◀ Small axes were used in both warfare and agriculture, but were increasingly relegated to the latter usage by large axes made specifically for battle. A small axe is depicted on the Bayeux Tapestry in the scene of the English shield wall, perhaps about to be used as a missile, The larger broad axe can be seen in comparison. That at lower left is probably of 12th-century date. (Museum of London)

◀ The broad axe was developed for war in about AD 1000. The blade was asymmetrical to assist a downward cut. The edge was made from specially hardened steel forged on to the blade. In section such axes are very thin, flaring suddenly to form an ovoid socket. They were mounted on a thick wooden haft about three feet long, though the Tapestry suggests even longer hafts were provided for ceremonial examples. (Reproduced by Courtesy of the Trustees of the British Museum)

Shields were made of wooden slats glued and nailed together, or of several layers with the grain of each placed at right angles like plywood. On circular shields an iron bar formed the handgrip, a hole being pierced in the middle of the shield for the knuckles and an iron boss riveted over it at the front. This example of c.900 from Gokstad in Norway is flat but many appear from illustrations to have been dished. The face might be covered in leather and the edges protected by leather or strips of iron or bronze. (University Museum of National Antiquities, Oslo. Photograph: L. Pedersen)

An English warrior wearing a long hauberk and conical helmet; his hand is resting on a round shield. This is from an 11th-century version of the Utrecht Psalter. Although this is essentially a copy of a 9th-century continental work, certain features such as the long hauberk, added later, indicate an eye for updating details. The new kite shield also appears in this manuscript. (By permission of the British Library, Harley MS.603 f73v)

◀ *The seax was a single-edged knife made by pattern welding; some had additional inlaid decoration. This example has the pointed back edge seen in the 10th and 11th centuries. The contemporary sheath is of leather tooled with decorative designs. The sheath was fastened over the front edge by rivets and was often worn horizontally at the belt with this side uppermost. Such knives were too short to be effective weapons except as a last resort and longer versions had dropped out of use by this time. Some may have been used particularly in the hunt. (Museum of London)*

a cutting edge of ten inches or more; it was mounted on a thick haft about three feet long, and was most effective when swung with both hands.

Some English flags appear on the Tapestry, together with two representations of the Dragon Banner of Wessex that flew over Harold's head-quarters. This was in effect a type of windsock shaped like a dragon with the muzzle (and possibly front legs) attached to the staff. Its origins lay in late Roman cavalry standards. Harold is also said to have had a personal flag, the Fighting Man, covered in gold threads and precious stones, on which was depicted the figure of a warrior.

There were few archers in the English ranks; a solitary figure is seen on the Tapestry. As a result, arrows were not shot in quantity and so there were few spent shafts for the Normans to re-use. There is little evidence that crossbows had as yet reached England. Slingers were probably numbered among the ranks of fyrdmen.

Harold's army appears to have been slightly larger than that of William, perhaps 8,000 men. At full strength the household troops of Harold and his two brothers numbered perhaps 1,000, but after the severe battle at Stamford Bridge their strength would have been reduced to something like 800 or less. However, conclusions are highly speculative. Supporting them were about 6,500 fyrdmen, the remainder possibly formed from men of the county militias of Sussex and perhaps Kent. Even 8,000 men would find the ridge at Hastings a rather cramped battlefield but this is in accord-ance with the remarks of contemporary chron-iclers.

▶ *The Viking warrior has a full mail coat and richly decorated sword. The low boss on his shield is typically Scandinavian. The Saxon ceorl wears a Phrygian cap of leather and carries a 'winged' spear. He may represent a free peasant provisioned by other members of a 5-hide unit, or a local militiaman. A well-armed but unarmoured English soldier appears on the hillock scene in the Bayeux Tapestry; most other sources also omit body armour. (G. A. Embleton)*

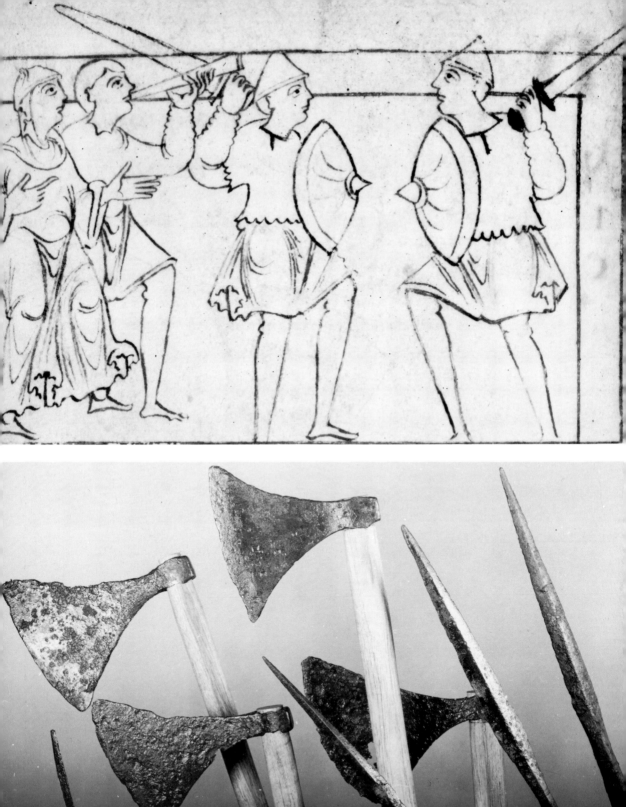

◀ *Early 11th-century warriors from an English 'Psychomachia', wearing short coats probably of mail but possibly of hide. To the early Germans it was a disgrace for a warrior to survive his lord on the battlefield, an epic ideal echoed in the 10th-century poem on the Battle of Maldon. Such notions of loyalty also infused the housecarls and thegns at Hastings. (By permission of The British Library, MS Cotton Cleopatra C.viii f18v)*

▶ *An unarmoured English thegn of c.1050 with conical helmet, shield and a sword suspended from a baldric. The lines across the shield may be metal reinforcing bands, the dots denote rivet heads for shield straps. Numerous figures are shown with no body armour other than some form of head protection. (By permission of The British Library, MS Cotton Tiberius C.vi f. 9)*

◀ *A group of early 11th-century spears and broad-axes found in the Thames near London Bridge and probably connected with Viking attacks on the city. This array gives an impression of how a line of English or Viking warriors would have looked, bristling with weapons. The hafts are modern. (Museum of London)*

# PLANS AND PREPARATIONS

## The Invasion Plan of Duke William

According to Wace, Duke William was out hunting when news of Harold's coronation reached him. A formal protest was sent to the new king, while the Norman cause, assisted by the formidable Hilde-brand (latterly Pope Gregory VII), was set out before Pope Alexander II. Here the Duke had a trump card. When Edward's Norman Archbishop of Canterbury had been expelled by Godwin the new primate was the earl's close associate, Stigand. The irregularity of his office, held in plurality with Winchester, together with the fact that successive popes refused this excommunicate the pallium, gave William the opportunity to plead that the English Church was in serious need of recon-struction. The Tapestry supports several Norman chroniclers who insist that Stigand presided at Harold's coronation; only John of Worcester asserts that in fact Harold took care to choose the respected Ealdred, Archbishop of York, but John came from the Worcester-York tradition and may be biased. At all events, Pope Alexander gave formal blessing and sent William a papal banner that was borne at Hastings, together with a ring containing a hair of Saint Peter, and which, according to Wace, William wore round his neck during the battle.

Politically, William's position was extremely favourable. His two greatest rivals, King Henry of France and Geoffrey, Count of Anjou, had both died in 1060. Henry's successor, Philip I, was a minor under the guardianship of William's father-in-law, Count Baldwin of Flanders. Anjou had lapsed into civil war. The buffer state of Maine had been occupied by the Normans in 1063, while thanks partly to the expedition of 1064 or 1065 there was a strong pro-Norman lobby in Brittany, so much so that the largest number of auxiliary troops came from this county. Count Eustace of Boulogne was friendly towards the Duke, and Ponthieu had been under his feudal suzerainty for twelve years. During the visit to Rome the Normans had also managed to ally with the German Emperor and with the Danes, who at this time were wary of Norway.

The Duke held a council at Lillebonne after receiving the papal banner, according to William of Malmesbury, and a second at Bonneville-sur-Touques (Orderic Vitalis, writing *c.*1109-25) where the provisioning of the ships was discussed. Feudal duty did not require service overseas and many were uninterested. Wace asserts that the council broke up in confusion, William resorting to individual interviews to wear down his vassals by dint of personality and the lucrative offers of lands in the conquered country. Many were at first opposed to attacking such a strong country, though it is possible that such stories were added to show William's foresight and persuasive powers in a good light. A third council was held at Caen in June. Meanwhile another sign was seen; the 'long-haired star' – Halley's Comet – appeared on 24 April and blazed in the sky for a week.

As soon as William had succeeded in per-suading his magnates to join him in his invasion of England he ordered ships to be found or built, perhaps a right based on the Scandinavian 'leid-angr' of his forebears. Possibly magnates with inland estates reimbursed ports that lay outside the lands of coastal lords. Specially built vessels may

*◀A northern French knight wears scale armour, which was occasionally used as an alternative to mail. Pieces of metal or horn were attached to an undershirt so that they overlapped downwards in the manner of the scales of a fish.*

*Some illustrations are so crude that the wavy lines depicted could represent mail or scale. The unarmoured squire may be a well-born youth undergoing training, or simply a servant. (Ed Dovey)*

have been of a standard size to lessen the problem of stragglers.

### Tostig's Raids

While these preparations were going on in Normandy, Harold's first opposition came from his own brother. Tostig, removed from his Northumbrian earldom in 1065, had wintered in Flanders, his wife, Judith, being half-sister to Count Baldwin. In early May he appeared with a fleet of 60 vessels off the Isle of Wight and began to ravage the south coast as far as Sandwich in Kent. Here he occupied the town and procured men and ships. It was now, according to *The Anglo-Saxon Chronicle*, that Harold first mobilized both the army and the fleet. On hearing of the royal forces marching from London, Tostig moved to Thanet where he met up with the exiled Copsi, who brought reinforcements from the Orkneys. The latter lay under Norwegian rule, suggesting that Tostig had already contacted the Norwegian court in order to ally with Harald Hardrada. According to Orderic Vitalis' interpolations of William of Jumièges, Tostig had also attempted to curry favour with

Duke William. Now the fleet sailed up the east coast, ravaging as it went. Rebuffed along the shores of Lindsey and Northumbria by Edwin and Morcar and deserted by ships and men, the remnant of twelve small ships finally sailed farther north where it passed the summer under the protection of Malcolm Canmore, King of Scotland. It was probably at this time that Tostig finally made his alliance with Harald Hardrada.

### The Invasion Force Gathers

By August the Norman fleet was taking shape and on the 4th or 5th the ships began to muster in the estuary of the river Dives at Dives-sur-Mer, with some at adjacent ports. The number of ships involved can only be estimated. Wace provides a figure of 696 from his father but qualifies it by saying that nobody even in the Conqueror's day knew the exact number. A much disputed ship list the original of which may possibly date from as early as 1067, gives a total of 776 provided by magnates. Possibly a small naval force already existed and further ships may have come from

*◄The skilled portrayal of the threatened King Harold, bowed on his precarious throne. Englishmen point in trepidation towards Halley's Comet, which visits the Earth every 75 years and blazed over England in April 1066. Such occurrences were seen as ominous portents of changes to come, here reinforced by the spectre of ghostly invasion ships gliding along in the lower border.*

Flemish naval mercenaries. Both sea-going long-ships (similar to the excellent vessels used by the Vikings) and deeper draughted cargo ships were probably provided. All were clinker built with overlapping strakes and propelled by a single large square sail. In order to manoeuvre when the mast was stepped or when becalmed, the ships could be rowed.

At Dives-sur-Mer Duke William set up a large camp, possibly covering more than 200 acres. As well as fighting men and horses there were squires, servants, sailors, cooks, armourers and butchers who dwelt in the camp for a month. William of Poitiers assures us that the Duke paid for every man's food so that the neighbouring herds and peasants were left unmolested. Given the exaggeration of the ducal panegyrist, it is still a notable achievement that William managed to keep together a host of perhaps 10,000 men for a month. It may be that he intended to cross the Channel from Dives; alternatively he might simply have wished to use the area as a holding base. The ships could be moored in the now vanished Gulf of Dives, safe from gales and also from raids by English ships. The area was ideally placed to receive corn supplies from the plain of Caen and was bordered by forests to provide timber for ships. It is possible that, rather than being held up at Dives for a month by northerly winds, as the chroniclers suggest, William deliberately delayed in order that the English fyrd who were guarding the coast would run out of provisions. William was well aware that Harold could muster a formidable force far superior to his own in numbers, and that any landing would be extremely risky. When an English spy was caught William showed him the Norman camp in a state of readiness; this would not only demonstrate his power but also persuade Harold that with an invasion imminent he must keep his men in arms.

The problems of sustaining the polyglot army at Dives were obvious. The fighting men not only had to be kept in order, but they and the warhorses needed to be maintained in peak condition. William's ability to keep his army fed may suggest that, aware of Roman and Byzantine military ideas, he ordered the construction of a large granary (not for fodder) in the camp. The filling of such a storehouse would have necessitated centralized control whereby provisions were purchased or requisitioned and then distributed. The 2,000 horses would have required approximately thirteen tons of grain and the same amount of hay per day, quite apart from the needs of the men, to which might be added wood and peat for cooking fires, and gallons of wine. Moreover there was the problem of disposing of large quantities of manure and urine; facilities would also have been necessary for the human element. Certainly the chroniclers do not mention any outbreak of disease among the army camped there that summer. The horses were probably stabled under timber lean-tos covered with branches and leaves, while mounted troops may have slept in hide tents each of which perhaps accommodated ten men.

## Harold's Dilemma

Since Tostig's attack, Harold had kept the army in readiness along the south coast. His failure to prepare adequately for an attack from Norway may have stemmed from a belief that the Normans would come first, or perhaps he preferred to protect his own southern lands and leave the defence of the north to Edwin and Morcar. The fleet took a long time to assemble, which may have resulted from the dismissal of a permanent nucleus by Edward the Confessor, leaving only the ship fyrd which had to be brought together. Harold meanwhile waited at Sandwich and, when the ships were assembled (perhaps 700 in number), he joined them and lay off the Isle of Wight. According to the 'E' version of *The Anglo-Saxon Chronicle*, Harold at some stage sailed out into the Channel searching for the Norman fleet. If the fyrd service at sea were for two months the fleet

# The Movements of Tostig and Harald Hardrada, 1066

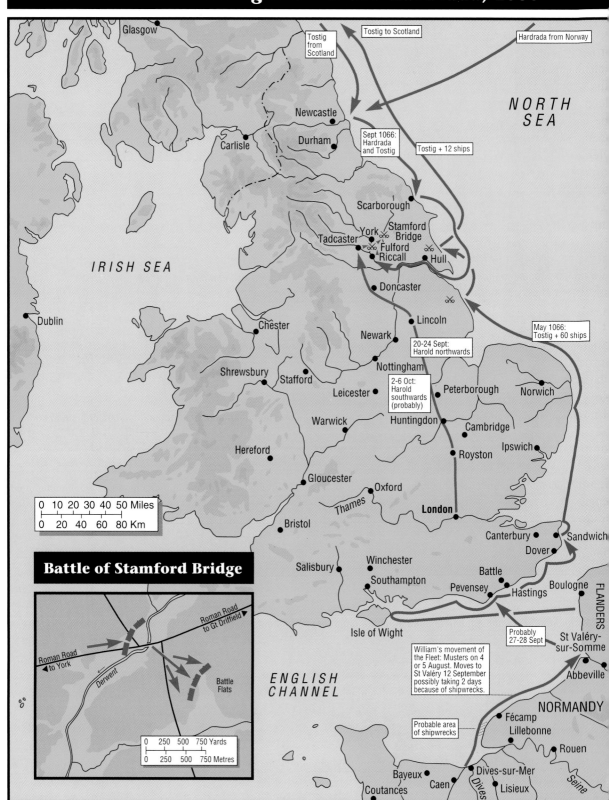

Tostig to Scotland

Hardrada from Norway

Glasgow

Tostig from Scotland

NORTH SEA

Newcastle

Sept 1066: Hardrada and Tostig

Carlisle

Durham

Tostig + 12 ships

Scarborough

York · Stamford Bridge

Tadcaster · Fulford

Riccall · Hull

IRISH SEA

Doncaster

Dublin

Lincoln

May 1066: Tostig + 60 ships

Chester

Newark

Shrewsbury

Stafford

Nottingham

20-24 Sept: Harold northwards

2-6 Oct: Harold southwards (probably)

Leicester

Peterborough

Norwich

Warwick

Huntingdon

Cambridge

Hereford

Royston

Ipswich

Gloucester

Oxford

Thames

London

Bristol

Canterbury

Sandwich

Dover

## Battle of Stamford Bridge

Salisbury

Winchester

Southampton

Battle

Pevensey

Hastings

Boulogne

FLANDERS

Isle of Wight

Probably 27-28 Sept

St Valéry-sur-Somme

0 10 20 30 40 50 Miles

0 20 40 60 80 Km

Roman Road to Gt Driffield

Roman Road to York

Derwent

Battle Flats

ENGLISH CHANNEL

William's movement of the Fleet: Musters on 4 or 5 August. Moves to St Valéry 12 September possibly taking 2 days because of shipwrecks.

Abbeville

NORMANDY

Fécamp

Lillebonne

0 250 500 750 Yards

0 250 500 750 Metres

Probable area of shipwrecks

Rouen

Bayeux

Caen

Dives-sur-Mer

Lisieux

Seine

Coutances

Dives

presumably returned to London at some time to change crews. This explains the length of time it remained on active service.

On 8 September the English army ran out of provisions and Harold, despite his gallant effort to hold it together for an unusual length of time, was finally forced to disband. The west wind having declined somewhat by this date, the King ordered the ships to London while he travelled on horseback. Highest water controlled the Atlantic current which suggests that Harold relied more on rowing to propel his ships; however, several vessels were lost through bad weather. William's organization had proved effective, and the English coast lay unprotected.

With the Channel now empty, William could move his invasion force more safely. After a month at Dives the pastureland was probably running out and he may have wished to move to a port that was closer to the proposed landing places of Pevensey and Hastings. So the Duke moved his forces eastwards to the port of Saint Valéry-sur-Somme some 160 miles along the coast in Vimeu, whose lord was related to both the houses of Normandy and Ponthieu. There was more chance of a southerly wind here and his ships would avoid the flood current waves of the Seine. Tidal conditions would have prevented such a move before 12 September, but westerly winds can be vigorous for about ten more days at this time of year. A departure between 03.00 and 04.00 GMT would have meant low water and high west winds. This move was not without mishap, for storms in the Channel wrecked several ships with consequent loss of life. If their sails were lowered the impaired directional control might have forced ships on to the cliffs between Cap de la Hève and Cap d'Antifer. The bodies were buried at night so as not to dishearten the troops. This may have meant the fleet arrived on the 14th. The horses were probably taken overland, a distance of about 100 miles; such a move would have been less traumatic and there is no mention of any losses in the chronicles.

## The Norse Invasion

As it happened, the first invasion of England came from the north. In the first week of September, while Harold was watching the south coast, Harald Hardrada of Norway made his bid for the English crown. Having mustered a fleet of between 300 and 500 ships, he sailed across the North Sea and was joined in the Tyne by Tostig who had come down from Scotland with additional ships. Together they sailed down the coast, plundering as they went, until they entered the Humber and moved up the Ouse as far as Riccall, ten miles from York. Here they set up camp before marching inland towards the city, most on foot, some on captured horses or ponies. At Gate Fulford, now a suburb, their way was blocked by a northern army raised by Earls Edwin and Morcar. There is no record of troop numbers; possibly between 5,000 and 6,000 men were involved on each side. The Earl of Orkney had accompanied Tostig, and the Norse army probably also included Scots, Englishmen and Flemish mercenaries. On Wednesday 20 September, the two armies clashed. The only description of the battle comes from the unreliable Icelandic poet, Snorri, though his description is not unlikely. Having marched along the river, the Norsemen formed on foot in line with their left flank resting on the river and their right on a ditch running parallel to it. Hardrada set up the Raven Banner, 'Land-ravager', near the river with his best warriors surrounding his giant frame. The English, also on foot in line, at first pushed back the poorer troops on the Norse right wing until Hardrada urged on his other warriors and broke up the enemy. Many Englishmen were drowned and Edwin and Morcar retreated. The battle had been bloody and costly in lives for both sides. Moreover, there was no question of the northern earls being able to supply Harold of England with fresh troops in the immediate future.

*◄ The Movements of Tostig and Harald Hardrada, May-September 1066. After landing at Sandwich, Tostig raided along the south and east coast until rebuffed in Lindsey and Northumbria, though it is not known precisely where. After Hardrada's invasion Harold marched up Ermine Street via Tadcaster and probably took the same road back again. Meanwhile William moved his fleet along the coast, losing some ships on the way, possibly between Cap de la Hève and Cap d'Antifer.*

*◀ The probable site of the battle of Gate Fulford, looking towards York. This is the view that would have been seen by the extreme left wing of Hardrada's army as it came upon the northern forces of Edwin and Morcar blocking the road to the city. The River Ouse winding towards York would have formed an effective defence for the flank of both armies.*

The Norsemen entered York and accepted its surrender. According to version 'C' of *The Anglo-Saxon Chronicle* (anti-Godwinist in tone) Hardrada arranged for them to join him in his march south, a comment that throws light on the differences that existed in England where much of the country was heavily settled by Scandinavians and by Englishmen of different tribal origins.

Harold first became aware of the Norwegian invasion when news of their landing reached him soon after his disbandment of the army on 8 September. Immediately he sent out a summons for the troops to gather, and in less than two weeks had decided to depart with the forces available. Advancing up the old Roman road from London he covered 190 miles in five days, reaching Tadcaster on the 24th. Having rested his men for the night, he marched through York on the morning of Monday 25 September, and out on to the road towards Stamford Bridge eight miles away, where the main Norse army was encamped as it waited for hostages from the surrounding countryside. The Vikings had no idea that a hostile army was in the vicinity; because of the fine weather many had left their armour at Riccall with the men detailed to guard the ships. According to Snorri, the first sight of Harold's army came from the cloud of dust on the York road. Through the cloud came the glint of armour and weapons; the saga says it was like the flash of sunlight on broken ice.

Stung into activity, Hardrada set about organizing his own men. He had little time, for the first sight of the enemy would have been from the crest of the hill at Gate Helmsley only one mile distant. Hardrada sent riders galloping the twelve miles back to Riccall with orders to the commander in charge of the troops there, Eyestein Orre, to come with all speed. The bulk of the invading army lay on the east bank of the River Derwent, but some were on the west bank in the path of the oncoming English host. A wooden bridge crossed the river about 400 yards upstream from the present bridge. The outposts on the west bank were given the grim task of holding off the English advance until the main force had armed and formed up on the slightly rising ground around Battle Flats. Having slain these defenders, Harold's troops pushed forward to the bridge. Here they were confronted by a lone Norseman who, because of the narrowness of the bridge, was able to fight off those who attacked him. Eventually an English soldier (possibly using a swill tub as a makeshift boat) manoeuvred himself beneath the bridge and thrust up with his spear, opening the way for the English army. The story only appears in English sources which suggests that there may be some truth in it.

Again there is little evidence for numbers involved although it is doubtful whether, given the casualties sustained by the invaders at Fulford and the speed with which Harold advanced, either army was of great size. The Norsemen were

▶ *The River Derwent at Stamford Bridge where a modern cut has made a new right-hand channel. In 1066 the bridge crossed the river at about this spot, approximately 400 yards upstream from the present bridge. The English army approached the far bank and only gained the bridge after fierce fighting with Norsemen protecting the main army as it formed up on the nearer side.*

▶ *Battle Flats at Stamford Bridge, the slightly rising ground where Harold Hardrada formed his men in a phalanx against the advancing army of Harold of England. This is the view obtained after crossing the River Derwent, whose wooden bridge was the only means of access to this bank.*

probably ordered into a circle (possibly a triangular formation). Hardrada is said to have fallen from his black horse when it stumbled while he was marshalling his troops but he simply remarked that a fall was lucky for a traveller. Snorri also tells how before battle commenced a group of twenty Norsemen rode from the English ranks. Tostig was offered Northumbria and a third of the kingdom if he submitted. When the earl asked what Hardrada would be granted he received the reply: seven feet of English ground, or as much more as he may be taller than other men. When Hardrada found out that Harold himself had delivered the message he said that, had he known, the King would never have been allowed to ride away.

Little is known of the progress of the battle, since Snorri's account seems to imply that the English attacked as cavalry and is suspiciously like the accounts of Hastings with the English in the place of Normans. In all likelihood it was a brutal infantry conflict that opened with archery and javelins (Snorri remarks that many Norsemen had brought bows) and soon became a hand-to-hand fight as the English sought to break up the Norse ring. Eventually Hardrada was mortally wounded by an arrow in the windpipe (recalling similarities with Harold at Hastings). Quarter was refused and as the battle resumed Eyestein Orre arrived from the ships. His men appear to have fought with almost berserker rage and the English suffered a setback. However, the newcomers had force-marched in armour and soon began to tire. Throwing aside armour and shield in a bid to continue fighting, many presented easy targets. As

◀ *A Norseman wearing a tough hide coat – which, it was said, could turn a blow as well as could mail. Viking dress was not too dissimilar from that worn in England, with some differences in style. The use of the axe demonstrates not only its cutting arc but its drawback in exposing the body to a thrust. (Ed Dovey)*

▶ *The Normans load their ships prior to embarking for England. Mail hauberks are carried on poles for ease of transport for if rolled up the weight is not distributed as it is when the coat is worn. One sword is slung by a wrist loop. Behind, men carry a cask together with what appears to be a dead pig. A large cask with bungs at both ends fills a cart together with spears and helmets. The latter are hooked over projections from the side bars and appear either to have solid neck guards as well as nasals or to show the nasals of two helmets together.*

evening approached, the invaders broke; many of their chiefs, including Hardrada and Tostig, were dead. Hardrada's son, Olaf, who had remained with the ships, was allowed to sail away in return for an oath of friendship. He needed only twenty-four ships to carry home the remnant of his army.

The English army had also suffered heavy casualties. Harold's jubilation was mixed with the knowledge that he had killed his brother (fratricide would be used latterly to fuel the Norman cause) and that the south lay unprotected. His worst fears were realized when, possibly during a victory feast on or shortly after 1 October, a messenger arrived with the news that William had landed in Sussex.

## The Norman Invasion

William had waited for the wind to back southerly, and vainly watched the weathercock on the church of Saint Valéry. In desperation he had the saint's relics brought from the church and paraded about, and the wind obligingly shifted direction. There is some dispute about the date of embarkation but it was probably 27 September. The ships would have had to be brought up to shore during high tide so that the horses could be embarked using ramps; High Tide was at 15.20. The army swarmed down

to the waiting ships in order to leave before low tide. Poitiers asserts that the fleet left before sunset, which suggests somewhere about 17.00. Low water in the Somme estuary has been estimated at 20.56 GMT and, because of the shallowness of the water at this time, the ships would have had to leave well before this, assisted by outflowing tidal currents. This would have allowed the fleet to reach Pevensey, 56 miles across the Channel from the estuary mouth, early the following morning. So as not to reach it until daylight, and to allow the ships to form up once beyond the Somme estuary, a short delay at anchor was necessary. Tidal streams caused a partial westerly curved sailing course for part of the way. William led the fleet in his own ship, the *Mora*, the gift of his wife. The prow bore the figure of a boy with an ivory trumpet. A lantern was slung high on the masthead as a guiding beacon, and the sound of a horn signalled the advance. Perhaps all had lanterns to prevent collisions, and probably sailed in staggered rows. The *Mora* was so swift that she pulled ahead of the rest and at dawn the Duke found himself alone in the Channel. Mindful of the morale of his men he ordered breakfast washed down with wine, as if in his own chamber at home, while he waited for the rest of the fleet to catch

▲ William's ship, the Mora, is distinguished by the boy with a horn set on the stern. There is a lantern at the masthead which was lit when the fleet had assembled at sea. The shields may have been placed along the low sides as protection from spray. The heads of war-horses can be seen in the ship on the right.

▼ Feudal warriors in mail hauberks are crammed in a ship, as depicted in the Life of St. Aubin from the monastery of St. Aubin at Angers. Although written c.1100, the armour and weapons shown are very similar to those of 1066. Notice here the annular mouldings around the spear sockets, which may explain so-called projections or 'wings' seen in many illustrations. (Bibliothèque Nationale MS Nouv.acq.lat.1390 f7r)

up. Gradually the forest of masts appeared and the fleet moved towards the coast of Sussex.

In 1066 Pevensey Bay consisted of a tidal lagoon separated from the sea by a shingle bank and set with small cultivated islands, which at low tide were separated by mud flats and water channels but possibly connected by causeways. On the western side of the bay a peninsula jutted into the lagoon, with a sheltered harbour behind. On this three-mile spit of land the Romans had built a stone fortress called Anderida, which by 1066 was partly ruinous. There was also the small town of Pevensey.

Probably at some time before 09.00 GMT (Low Water was at about 09.20) the first Norman vessels arrived at the lagoon. They would have had to negotiate a large gap in the shingle bank and manoeuvre past the mud flats until they came into the harbour under the north wall of the fort, where

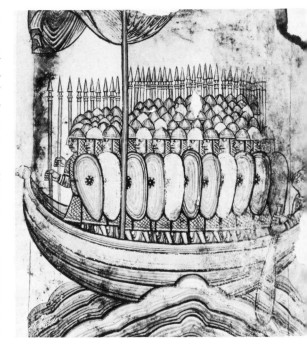

▶ *Skuldelev Wreck 3, a small trader with forward and aft decks, built c.930-1130 and measuring 13.8 metres long with a beam of 3.4 metres. Such a ship could have carried provisions across the Channel, the cargo stored in the centre and covered with skins to protect it from spray. Only five or six men would have been needed to crew her.*

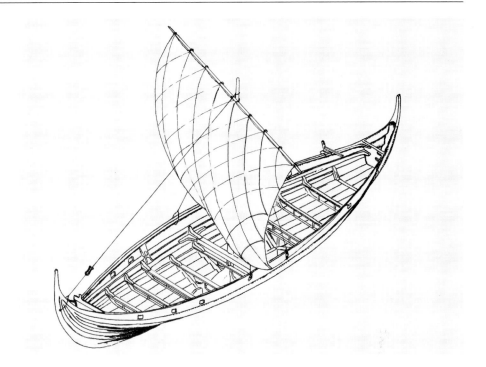

▶ *A section through Skuldelev Wreck 1, showing the open central area for holding provisions or livestock and the raised decks forward and aft.*

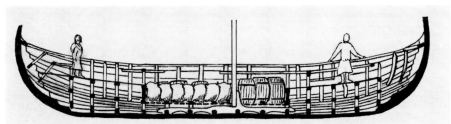

▶ *Skuldelev Wreck 1, recovered from the bed of Roskilde Fjord in Denmark and dating from between c.910 and c.1110. A trading vessel, 16.3 metres long with a beam of 4.5 metres, forward and after decks left a central area for cargo. Such ships would have been sturdy and stable enough to transport both horses and provisions across the Channel and would have needed only about four or five men to handle them. Being of similar construction to warships, these vessels too could probably be beached to allow the horses to be jumped from the decks. (Viking Ship Museum, Roskilde, Denmark)*

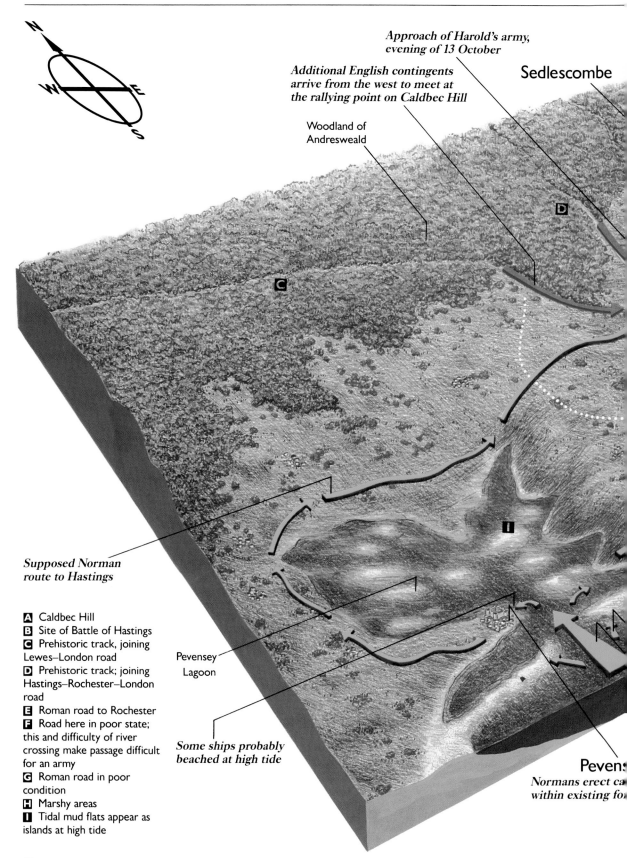

*Approach of Harold's army,
evening of 13 October*

*Additional English contingents
arrive from the west to meet at
the rallying point on Caldbec Hill*

Sedlescombe

Woodland of
Andresweald

**C**

**D**

**I**

*Supposed Norman
route to Hastings*

**A** Caldbec Hill
**B** Site of Battle of Hastings
**C** Prehistoric track, joining
Lewes–London road
**D** Prehistoric track; joining
Hastings–Rochester–London
road
**E** Roman road to Rochester
**F** Road here in poor state;
this and difficulty of river
crossing make passage difficult
for an army
**G** Roman road in poor
condition
**H** Marshy areas
**I** Tidal mud flats appear as
islands at high tide

Pevensey
Lagoon

*Some ships probably
beached at high tide*

Peven

Pevens
Normans erect ca
within existing for

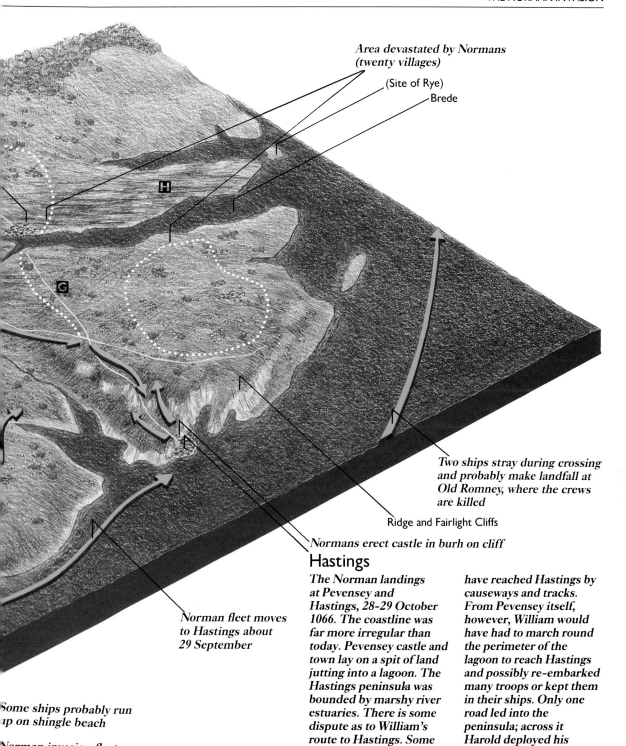

Area devastated by Normans
*(twenty villages)*

(Site of Rye)

Brede

H

G

Two ships stray during crossing
and probably make landfall at
Old Romney, where the crews
are killed

Ridge and Fairlight Cliffs

Normans erect castle in burh on cliff

Norman fleet moves
to Hastings about
29 September

Some ships probably run
up on shingle beach

Norman invasion fleet
about 8-9 a.m., 28 September
from St. Valéry)

## Hastings

The Norman landings
at Pevensey and
Hastings, 28-29 October
1066. The coastline was
far more irregular than
today. Pevensey castle and
town lay on a spit of land
jutting into a lagoon. The
Hastings peninsula was
bounded by marshy river
estuaries. There is some
dispute as to William's
route to Hastings. Some
forces may have
disembarked along the
shingle bank and could
have reached Hastings by
causeways and tracks.
From Pevensey itself,
however, William would
have had to march round
the perimeter of the
lagoon to reach Hastings
and possibly re-embarked
many troops or kept them
in their ships. Only one
road led into the
peninsula; across it
Harold deployed his
forces when William
marched to meet him.

# THE NORMAN LANDINGS
## at Pevensey and Hastings, 28-29 September 1066

there were probably wharves. It seems likely that the Duke's ship, those carrying the horses and the soldiers designated for a garrison at Pevensey would have been landed here. By Low Water the level had dropped twenty feet, allowing ships to be beached on the muddy flats so exposed. Some chroniclers mention that disembarkation took place at intervals along the shore, or that the shore was seized. Although one need not attach too much importance to this, it is possible that many ships ran up on to the shingle bank.

Although writing a century later, Wace gives a good impression of what may have been the tactical debarkation; archers jumped down from the ships with strung bows in order to cover their fellows. Behind them, armed knights began to leave the ships and form up to deal with any opposition. There was none; the men began to pour out of the vessels. William of Malmesbury, followed by Wace, tells the story of how William fell as he stepped ashore, but that the potentially bad omen was turned to good effect when a nearby knight remarked how the Duke had the earth of England in his hands. The horses were probably made to jump into the shallows.

Once disembarked the Normans busied themselves in fortifying the Roman remains by cutting off one corner with a ditch and timber defences. However, William decided to move eastwards along the coast to Hastings. Why he initially

◀ *The mast is unstepped as one of the ships arrives at Pevensey. The Tapestry was considered rather unhelpful in answering the question of how the horses were disembarked, since they are shown simply stepping from the ships on to dry land.*

▲ *In 1963 Danish Scouts, using a replica of the 9th-century Ladby ship, built in 1935, conducted experiments in the transportation of horses. This ship was a warship with an extremely shallow draught. From its low* *sides, horses could be jumped easily on to a quay or into shallows in a similar way to that shown in the Bayeux Tapestry. But the ship was not tried at sea, where the very shallow draught would probably have made her unstable and dangerous for horses. An alternative suggestion is that very large warships were used to transport the animals, with additional decking, stalls and ramps. Such ships could also carry large quantities of stores. (Viking Ship Museum, Roskilde, Denmark)*

landed at Pevensey is not known for certain. Perhaps he was attracted by the lagoon; perhaps the fleet was swept too far west by cross-currents. Two vessels had been separated, probably landing at Old Romney to be dispatched by the inhabitants. Probably while at Pevensey William and 25 knights had searched unsuccessfully for a passage presumably across the mud-flats, for the distance around the perimeter of the lagoon was 26 miles and there was no serviceable road eastwards from Pevensey. If landings had taken place on the east of the shingle bank, William perhaps ordered the march to Hastings the same day and may not even have disembarked part of his cavalry, but let it pass down the coast instead.

The Saxon town now lies under water in the area of the pier. In 1066 there was a high peninsula where William set up camp. His men erected a timber castle, possibly within the Saxon burh on

▼ *The Roman walls of Anderida were built at Pevensey on a peninsula jutting into a lagoon which has now been reclaimed. Only the gate on the right gave access to the small town and the mainland. On landing here in September 1066, William put a ditch and palisade across the opposite corner, utilizing the existing Roman walls. Wace recounts that preformed timbers were brought across in ships. The later medieval castle was built in the same corner, and the foundations of the Anglo-Saxon church also lie within the fortress. (Cambridge University Collection; copyright reserved)*

▶ *The Normans erect a motte at Hastings. The area may in fact have been a palisaded enclosure with ditch and rampart, for the English designer may have assumed that it was another motte of the type being built in the newly conquered country. Notice the rammed layers, used in the raising of some mottes, though the mound at Hastings castle is not constructed in this way.*

the hill. Foragers were sent out and scouts posted to warn of enemy approach.

By moving to Hastings William showed that he intended to approach London via the road to Dover because the route through Chichester along the South Downs would have meant starting from Pevensey. The entire area of the Hastings peninsula made a secure base as it was difficult of access to an army. To the west was the Bulverhythe lagoon, to the east the marshy valleys of the rivers Brede and Rother, which curved round northwards towards the great forest called the Andredsweald, which was cut by boggy streams and local tracks. A Roman road, probably much neglected, ran from Rochester through the forest and necessitated fording the Brede to reach Hastings. However, a track passed between the watercourses and out of the peninsula to meet the road farther north-east. Although William could reach London from Rochester, the Norman cavalry would have been at a serious disadvantage by using a route that passed through woodland. Alternatively, he could turn eastwards to Dover and the coastal route.

William could have struck out for London in the hope of securing it before Harold returned from the north but a march inland or along the coast might have allowed Harold to sever his lines of communication. By staying in the peninsula with

*▲ The castle perched on the heights above Hastings. Much of the cliff later fell down before the sea began to recede. To the right of the remains of the church the curtain wall crosses a mound which may enclose William's motte. The church was probably standing in the Iron Age ruins when William arrived. The harbour lay to the west at the foot of Castle Hill, which probably jutted into the sea, (Cambridge University Collection; copyright reserved)*

only one road out and a constricted entrance, he had a secure base. Neither did William wish to tarry for long. As they set up camp the Duke was approached by a messenger from a kinsman settled in England, Robert, son of the lady Guimora. He informed the Duke of Harold's great victory in the north and advised him to remain within entrenchments and not to offer battle. However, William had everything to gain by forcing a confrontation

*▶ Anglo-Danish housecarl and English fyrdman returning from Stamford Bridge. The paucity of representations of English armour is only offset by occasional references, such as the helmet and corselet expected from every eight hides from the 'E' version of The Anglo-Saxon Chronicle for 1008. Housecarls and thegns rode, using stirrups ultimately derived from Viking types. The byrnie is rolled up and slung behind the saddle but could also be carried on a supply wagon. (Ed Dovey)*

in the open, where he could use his cavalry to best effect. Otherwise the English fleet might well cut off an escape to sea and Harold could block the road to London, seal the Normans in the Hastings peninsula and wait until their supplies ran out, while the English army increased in strength. Knowing this, and knowing Harold's temperament from his meeting probably in 1064, William deliberately set about devastating the surrounding area in an endeavour to lure him to battle. Sussex lay in Harold's old earldom and such destruction was an insult to his lordship. It also brought William fresh supplies.

Meanwhile Harold lost no time in mustering his men and marching back south. In five days he reached London, where he waited impatiently for his army to reorganize and for fresh troops to arrive. A monk took a formal message to William (probably also to spy the camp) and a Norman monk from Fécamp was sent back with a response,

rejecting any deathbed nomination of Harold by Edward, offering to take the matter to litigation or, failing that, settling the question by single combat. Wace makes the King's brother, Gyrth, suggest that Harold decline battle but ravage to deny provisions to the enemy before allowing Gyrth to risk a battle. Harold refuses to hurt his own people and insists on leading the army himself. In some ways the idea is sound; certainly by waiting Harold would grow stronger in numbers while William would become more desperate. However, Harold waited only five or six days in London, probably until the 11th, before setting out with the troops at his disposal. He marched between 50 and 60 miles, moving through the Andredsweald to arrive on the evening of 13 October at Caldbec Hill, where stood the assembly point called the Hoar Apple Tree, one mile from the forest edge. The London road via Rochester or Dover together with that via Lewes and Chichester met close by here

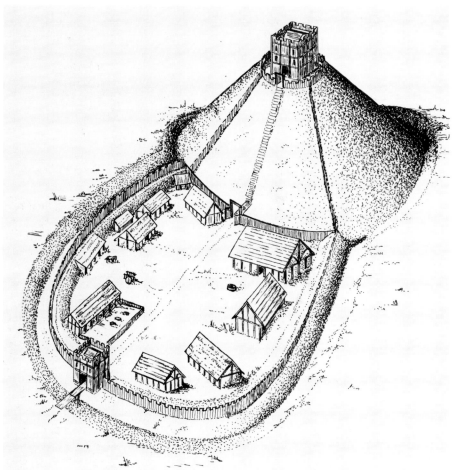

◀ *A reconstruction of a motte and bailey castle, based on John Banbury's illustration of Rhuddlan, built in 1073. Many early earth and timber castles may have been fortified enclosures without a mound. Stables, storerooms, smithy, animal houses, sheds and a well would have been placed in the bailey or courtyard. A hall also would have been sited here if there were no motte or if the latter were very small.*

before continuing the eight miles to Hastings. It is usually assumed that the King intended to surprise William as he had surprised Hardrada and attack his camp (perhaps even at night) as Poitiers asserts. It is also possible, however, that Harold may have wanted to bottle up the Normans in the Hastings peninsula to contain them until the English army had grown in strength; Poitiers mentions 700 ships sent to deny any withdrawal by sea. In the event Harold was given no choice, for it was William who moved first.

Norman scouts, seven miles from Hastings, came galloping back during daylight with news that the English army was marching south. William ordered the whole camp to stand to arms and foragers were called in. The camp remained at arms all night in case of attack, while the priests heard confessions throughout the hours of darkness. William of Malmesbury and latterly Wace contrast this piety with the English carousing the night away, but since they had just completed a hurried march this seems extremely implausible.

*Norman foragers fire a house. Ravaging was a normal facet of feudal warfare, bringing supplies and loot without great danger and being an insult to the lord who was supposed to be able to protect his property. When his forces appeared, the foragers would withdraw. Here, however, William needed a confrontation to open the way to the throne, and he was deliberately luring Harold south.*

*A windmill now stands on Caldbec Hill north of the battlefield at Hastings. It was in this vicinity, the site of the Hoar Apple Tree, that Harold mustered his men before marching down to the ridge beyond. It was an ideal rallying point because four roads met here.*

# THE BATTLE

Before daybreak on Saturday, 14 October, William heard Mass, took the Sacrament and hung round his neck the sacred relics on which Harold had sworn his oath. A waning moon, twenty-two days old, hung in the sky as dawn broke at about 05.20; the sun rose at 06.48 and it was reported that the morning was unusually light. William was determined to meet Harold in the open field and to strike first. The column moved out of the encampment and made its way along the Roman road as it wound northwards towards the great forest of Andredsweald. If the Normans had camped on the Baldslow Ridge above Hastings town and the column had begun its march at about 06.00, the head of the column could have reached Telham Hill in about an hour. The summit, now called Blackhorse Hill, was known as Hecheland; here William probably called a halt while his troops began to don their armour. As the Duke put on his hauberk those around were disturbed to see that it was reversed to the left, but William laughed off any idea of a bad omen. William of Poitiers carefully reports the gist of the Duke's pep-talk to his men, but considering the column could have wound back several miles it is more likely that his words were addressed to his immediate commanders. The Tapestry shows a knight called Vital, one of Bishop Odo's vassals, informing the Duke that the enemy had been sighted. The spot from which this would have been possible is somewhere about the 300 contour line, only 800 yards from the enemy. At the same time, armed English scouts reported the enemy to Harold.

From Caldbec Hill the London to Hastings road passed along a neck of land until it reached a broad ridge that opened out each side. The entire site was like a hammer, the head forming a ridge approximately 800 yards in length. In front of the ridge, the ground sloped down into what appeared to be a valley, but in fact was a saddle of land between the headwaters of two brooks with marshy banks that cut across it. The road crossed the saddle between these brooks and climbed the slopes of Telham Hill in the direction of Hastings, seven miles away. It was along this ridge that Harold now deployed his troops, completely blocking the road to London. The ground sloping south from the ridge was called Santlache ('Sandy Stream') by the English, later to be punned as Senlac ('Blood Lake') by the Normans. This and the eastern slope may have been cultivated but the flanks dropped sharply, with a gradient of about one in twelve (one in four at the rear), while the thick undergrowth and the woody nature of the area added to the difficulty of a flank attack. William had little alternative to a frontal assault uphill. Near the road the gradient is about one in fifteen, the gentlest slope, one in 33, being at the western end. North of the western brook, a low hillock rose about fifteen feet. Although the position was a strong one for Harold's infantry, it was nevertheless crowded. Poitiers says there was scarcely room for the wounded to leave, while John of Worcester asserts that many deserted because of the constrained position. The only retreat lay along the neck of land to the rear. William was equally ill-served, however. Although the bottleneck had meant that he could be relatively sure of the direction of an enemy attack, the hill position and constricted space was not ideal for cavalry

*◄ Norman infantrymen wearing hauberks. According to William of Poitiers, the Norman infantry wore 'loricatos', a term that in the 11th century denoted mail. This is supported by a few depictions of them on the Bayeux Tapestry. However, not all infantry would carry kite shields, and the circular variety continued in use with foot soldiers both in England and Normandy. Poitiers notes the use of javelins at Hastings. (Nigel Longdon)*

action that was further hampered by the marshy ground around the streams on the valley floor.

William had out-generalled Harold and struck first. Contemporaries agree that the King was himself caught by surprise before his army was fully assembled, the penalty for concentrating his forces within striking distance of the enemy. It has been suggested that passages in the *Carmen* imply that William used hand-signals to recall knights perhaps stationed at advanced outposts on Telham Hill, and that Norman archers and crossbowmen were sent ahead of the main body in a vain attempt to prevent Harold's seizure of the ridge, although the number of English troops in the vicinity would have made this difficult. However, William had now forced a battle and must win it to survive.

Harold placed his standard on the highest point of the ridge. Out in front, his army formed up in a fairly level line extending along the ridge

▲ The Norman view of the ridge west of Harold's headquarters, as seen today. The ground has been altered to accommodate William's abbey. The cellars of the guesthouse roughly follow the line of the English position and the ground behind has been built up.

◄ The English view of the Norman positions in the valley below, with Telham Hill in the background. Seen from the centre, William and his Norman division would have attacked here. To the extreme right can be seen the low hump of the hillock where Bretons and Englishmen came to grief.

▼ *Part of the battlefield of Hastings. The Abbey is in the right foreground; the twin towers of Princess Elizabeth's Lodging mark the approximate line of the English position running towards the centre foreground. Harold's headquarters was at the right corner. The Breton division was set in front of the hillock, whose position is roughly marked by the clump of trees between the fishpond and the Abbey. The line of trees extending from the pond towards the foreground indicates the Asten Brook. (Cambridge University Collection; copyright reserved)*

# The Battle of Hastings:
# Preliminary Positions at about 9am, 14 October 1066

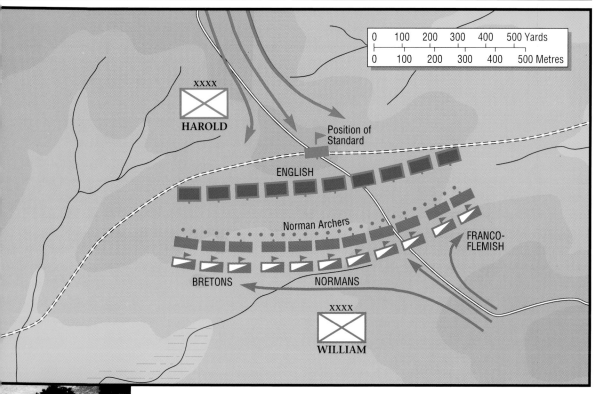

| 0 | 100 | 200 | 300 | 400 | 500 Yards |
| 0 | 100 | 200 | 300 | 400 | 500 Metres |

XXXX
HAROLD

Position of
Standard

ENGLISH

Norman Archers

FRANCO-
FLEMISH

BRETONS    NORMANS

XXXX
WILLIAM

▲ *The Battle: preliminary positions at about 09.00 hours, 14 October 1066. Having reached Caldbec Hill on the 13th, Harold moved down to place his standard on the highest point of the ridge the following morning. The army consisted of perhaps 8,000 infantry in about ten ranks, the best troops in front. A bodyguard of housecarls and king's thegns guarded the king. William's force of perhaps 7,500 was divided into Bretons on the left, Normans in the centre and Franco-Flemish on the right. It was divided into three lines: archers in front, heavy infantry (who probably made up the largest proportion) behind and cavalry in rear.*

for about 800 yards, the King's own position being somewhere near the centre of its length. Some authorities consider that the line was up to 200 yards shorter at the eastern end. William of Malmesbury says that Harold's brothers, Gyrth and Leofwine, were with him, but since they were killed fairly early it seems more likely they were in the line, perhaps on the left and right. This further strengthens the idea that the best troops provided by the three brothers formed the front ranks rather than surrounding Harold, as some have suggested. But a bodyguard would have been held back to protect the King and the standards. Behind the well-armed and armoured warriors in the line stood the lesser thegns and in rear the unarmoured levies of the militia drawn largely from Sussex and perhaps Kent. The whole presented a phalanx perhaps ten ranks deep, the slope of the hill allowing Harold to look over the heads of his men, It has been suggested that the wings of the army were bent back although this would have served little purpose other than to place some men on lower ground. As Harold and his commanders marshalled the men now streaming across the neck of land to join the troops along the ridge, they watched the leading contingents of the Norman forces begin to descend the slopes of Telham Hill and move towards the saddle between the streams.

In order to form up at the bottom of the slope the Normans had to follow the road past the saddle between the streams. It is generally thought that, because of the boggy nature of ground in the vicinity of the streams, which consists of heavy clay, the army passed the saddle in column before spreading out to form up in line. This would necessitate deploying almost within bowshot of the enemy, but perhaps William believed that Harold would not sacrifice his position to risk a sudden onslaught. It is just possible, however, that a long spell of dry weather might have rendered the ground sufficiently hard to allow deployment short of the saddle and a subsequent advance in line.

The first troops reached the saddle at about 08.00 hours. The Bretons, who formed the largest non-Norman contingent, together with men from Anjou, Poitou and Maine, wheeled left and took up position at the western end of the valley probably under Alan Fergant of Brittany, a cousin of the ruling count and William's son-in-law. A low hillock north of the Asten Brook stood at their rear. On their right the Norman division, the largest, took position with the Duke in the middle. At his side Turstin, son of Rollo, bore the papal banner, and around him were friends and kinsmen. At the eastern end of the valley, forming the smallest division, were the contingents from France, Picardy, Boulogne and Flanders under the seneschal, William fitzOsbern, and Count Eustace of Boulogne. With them was young Robert of Beaumont, whose first battle this was. Each division or 'battle' was separated into three parts. In the front line stood the archers and probably crossbowmen and a few slingers, mostly unarmoured. Behind, though not seen on the Bayeux Tapestry, were the infantry, many wearing mail coats. Behind stood squadrons of cavalry. From these dispositions it can be seen that William envisaged a pattern of attack. The archers would first soften up the English line with a barrage of arrows. This would be followed by an assault with his heavy infantry who would force gaps in the line. Finally his best troops, the knights on their costly chargers, would break up the defence and pursue the defeated enemy. Bishop Odo is not now thought to have participated in the actual fighting. Like Bishop Geoffrey of Coutances he probably sent prayers for divine help, and helped marshal and encourage the men. On the lower slopes of Telham Hill stood the priests together with servants, boys who, says Wace, were not expected to involve themselves in the fighting.

Across the valley on the ridge above, the English watched. They had formed their 'shield wall', a term that has posed great problems of interpretation. It finds mention in the 10th century poem on the battle of Maldon, and on the Tapestry the line of English troops are shown with their shields overlapping. The comparison of the English phalanx to a castle by Henry of Huntingdon (writing c.1125) together with a confused passage in Wace, led the Victorian writer Freeman to assume that a palisade had been built before the English line, an idea ridiculed by his opponent Round. The shield wall or war hedge was formed by the front ranks holding their shields close together. Initially, as on the Tapestry, they may have been overlapped, for which the warriors would have had to stand sideways. In this form would have been an effective barrier against missiles. However, this formation would have had to be broken up in order to wield weapons in close combat, especially the great double-handed axe that needed room to be swung.

Wace describes the English war cries, 'Olicrosse!', (Holy Cross!) and 'Godemite!' (God Almighty) as well as the chant, 'Ut, ut', (Out, out). They probably also beat their shields, all resulting in a martial din designed as much to bolster their own spirits as to frighten the enemy.

A story is told by the *Carmen*, Henry of Huntingdon and Wace that a minstrel rode before the Duke. His name was Taillefer (lit. 'Cut Iron') and he juggled with his sword and sang the Song of Roland, the epic of the well-known Frankish hero. Granted permission to strike the first blow he galloped forward and attacked a group of Englishmen who had presumably left the line

CON·RA·AN GLO

*The Norman archers opened the battle. Their ranks included crossbowmen and probably slingers, not shown on the Tapestry, The full armour of one figure would have been very rare and may denote captain. Arrows are here held in the left hand ready to be loaded, an unlikely*

*practice in reality. Archaeological evidence suggests that bows were often almost six feet long; if they were as powerful as longbows their range of about 300 yards would mean that the armies would have been within continual bowshot of each other.*

meet him. Felling one with his lance and then another with his sword, he was soon surrounded and cut down. The story may or may not be true. William of Malmesbury mentions the singing of the Song of Roland but omits mention of Taillefer.

The battle began at the third hour, that is, approximately 09.00 GMT, and was signalled by the terrible sound of trumpets. It is worth recalling the remark of Freeman that medieval battles all

seem to begin in accordance with church hours. The ranks of Norman and allied archers and crossbowmen moved forward. The opening barrage hissed up the slopes but proved singularly ineffective. Given the angle of trajectory and the slope of the hill, many of the arrows were caught on the shields of the troops in the front line. Missiles that were shot higher simply passed over the heads of the entire army to fall harmlessly behind, though a few stray shafts may have struck latecomers arriving in rear of the English line. There were few archers among the English; the Tapestry portrays a solitary figure. Many, lacking horses, had not managed to keep up with Harold's march south. Others were presumably killed at the battles of Fulford and Stamford Bridge. With few archers, there were correspondingly few arrows to be retrieved and re-used by the Normans in their turn. Their quivers, each of which probably held about 24 arrows (the later medieval 'sheaf') would

have been emptied in a few minutes, and even if additional supplies had been brought up on supply carts they were presumably inadequate, since the archers do not appear to have made much impression at this stage but would appear again later. The first phase of William's assault had failed; the enemy line was intact.

William now sent his other infantry toiling up the slopes against the unbroken English line. As they advanced they were met by a hail of missiles that included arrows, javelins and slingstones. Poitiers notes axes, by which he probably means the smaller, Danish axe, and stones lashed to pieces of wood. The Tapestry even shows a mace in flight. The Normans recoiled but pressed on again and at last closed with the English. The lines swayed as the invaders strove to break through the enemy ranks. This brutal struggle went on for some time until William, realizing that his infantry could make no headway, ordered squadrons of cavalry to advance in support. The clash of weapons, the shrieks of wounded men and horses, together with the shouting and chanting of those at the rear must have been appalling as the knights spurred their horses towards the mêlée. As they did so, they too were struck by missiles that tumbled them to the ground or maddened their horses; however, the cavalry squadrons came on, their speed slowed by the slope of the hill.

Contingents of knights followed the pennon of their lord as they swept up the hill, drawing their swords or in some cases perhaps a mace if the lance were lost, seeking a gap in the shields or the moment when an axe was raised and allowed a thrust to be delivered. The horsemen did not stand still but rode up and away, returning to re-engage. The English stoutly resisted and even wounded those Norman infantrymen who were throwing javelins from a distance. Poitiers points out how the English were helped by the slope, by their close order and by the effectiveness of their weapons. The great axes cleft shields and a well-aimed blow apparently could slice through horse and rider together.

◀ *A housecarl wearing a long mail coat, and a thegn in the older style of corselet; each could equally wear the other. In the same way, either the kite shield or the traditional circular variety was carried. On the Bayeux Tapestry both sides are depicted in similar armour, and it is possible that the English workmanship suggests that predominantly English dress is shown. The banner of the Dragon of Wessex was essentially a windsock of a type that can be traced back to Roman and Sarmatian standards. (Ed Dovey)*

▼ *The English 'shield wall'. The Tapestry shows the line composed predominantly of the more important warriors, mailed housecarls and king's thegns. This is probably the reason so few Norman infantrymen figure in the Tapestry, except where they are necessary to the story. The large broad axe at left contrasts with the smaller Danish axe on the right. The overlapping shields may have stopped missiles, but for close fighting the formation would have had to be broken up to allow the two-handed axes to be swung. Notice the lone English archer on the right, and the men holding bundles of javelins.*

## The Crisis

The toll of dead and wounded began to affect the Bretons and other auxiliaries on the left of the line. At last they could take it no longer; the foot-soldiers and cavalry broke and fled back down the slope. This dangerously exposed William's flank. The Normans in the centre began to pull back partly out of prudence and partly because of the panic that was spreading along the ranks. Even the French and Flemish on the right wing began to be affected. Rumour spread that Duke William had been killed. It was an extremely serious moment, for Englishmen on the right of their position were now running down the hill in pursuit of the Bretons. A number of their knights rode over the hillock that had been at their backs when deployed in line. Now, urging their horses over the top, some plunged floundering into the stream on the southern side, while other fugitives were slowed by the neighbouring marshy ground. The pursuing Englishmen began to catch up and lash out at the struggling Bretons.

It was now that William reacted swiftly. In order to stifle the rumour of his death he took off or pushed back his helmet so that all might see his face, no longer obscured by the broad nasal guard.

The Tapestry shows Eustace of Boulogne, who has seized the papal banner, frantically pointing to the Duke as he rides through his troops. William roaring that he was alive, reminded his men that there was no escape except to the sea and a waiting English fleet. Meanwhile his half-brother, Odo seeing the débâcle from his place in the rear galloped up to confront and rally a number of young panic-stricken warriors who were riding towards the slopes of Telham Hill. William, sizing up the situation on the left wing, led a body of knights – Wace rather grandly suggests a body guard of 1,000 men – across the field down to where Englishmen were fighting on the marsh ground. The horsemen, coming partially down the slopes, rode through them and cut down their unarmoured opponents. Some managed to clam

▶ *William pushes back his helmet and shows his face as the rumour spreads that he has fallen. The angle of the helmet shows that it was secured in position with laces under the chin. The Duke has mail undersleeves and leggings; the latter were sometimes strapped over* *the front of the leg. Count Eustace of Boulogne is sporting a moustache, which may have been added later. He is grasping what is almost certainly the papal banner, though his presence during the incident may be propagandist.*

▲ Some of the best artistry on the Tapestry portrays the horses of the fleeing Bretons floundering in the marshy ground behind the hillock. The unarmoured English levies who had driven them back to this place are themselves trapped by Normans from the central division. The English peasants mostly have only spear and shield, which agrees with evidence in early 11th-century wills.

▲ The hillock over which the Bretons fled and on to which the Normans drove their English pursuers is marked by the clump of trees to the left of centre, which also highlights the slope of the hill. The bushes at the extreme left mark the marshy stream, later partly turned into abbey fishponds.

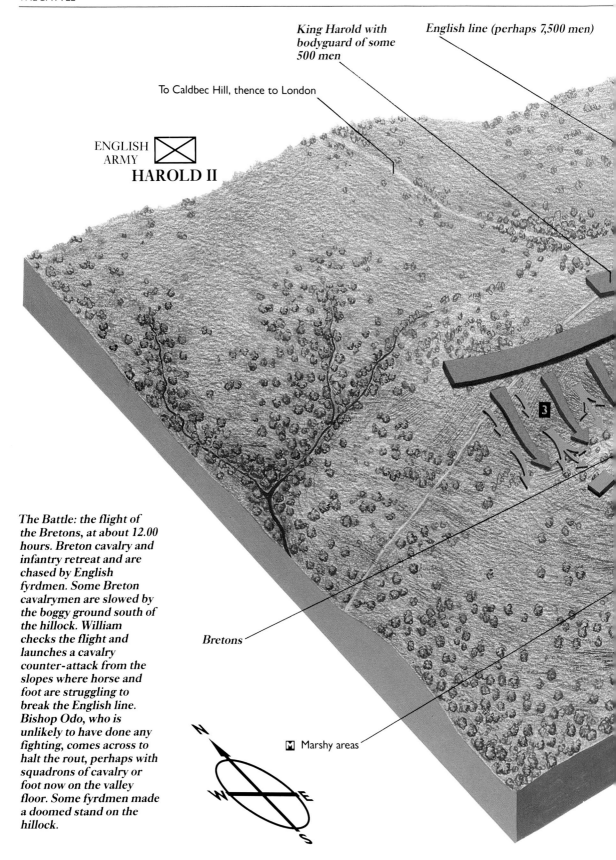

King Harold with bodyguard of some 500 men

English line (perhaps 7,500 men)

To Caldbec Hill, thence to London

ENGLISH ARMY

# HAROLD II

*The Battle: the flight of the Bretons, at about 12.00 hours. Breton cavalry and infantry retreat and are chased by English fyrdmen. Some Breton cavalrymen are slowed by the boggy ground south of the hillock. William checks the flight and launches a cavalry counter-attack from the slopes where horse and foot are struggling to break the English line. Bishop Odo, who is unlikely to have done any fighting, comes across to halt the rout, perhaps with squadrons of cavalry or foot now on the valley floor. Some fyrdmen made a doomed stand on the hillock.*

Bretons

Ⓜ Marshy areas

N
W  E
S

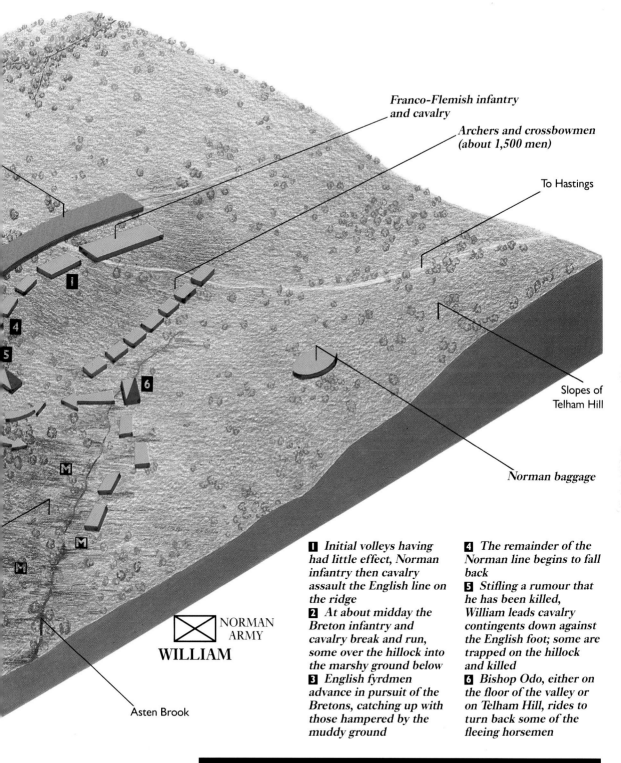

Franco-Flemish infantry
and cavalry

Archers and crossbowmen
(about 1,500 men)

To Hastings

Slopes of
Telham Hill

Norman baggage

NORMAN
ARMY

WILLIAM

Asten Brook

**1** Initial volleys having
had little effect, Norman
infantry then cavalry
assault the English line on
the ridge
**2** At about midday the
Breton infantry and
cavalry break and run,
some over the hillock into
the marshy ground below
**3** English fyrdmen
advance in pursuit of the
Bretons, catching up with
those hampered by the
muddy ground

**4** The remainder of the
Norman line begins to fall
back
**5** Stifling a rumour that
he has been killed,
William leads cavalry
contingents down against
the English foot; some are
trapped on the hillock
and killed
**6** Bishop Odo, either on
the floor of the valley or
on Telham Hill, rides to
turn back some of the
fleeing horsemen

# THE BATTLE OF HASTINGS

**The flight of the Bretons and the Norman counterattack,
about midday 14 October 1066, as seen from the south**

ber up the hillock and make a forlorn stand against the milling horsemen but the latter closed in and wiped them out. The crisis had passed.

It has been suggested that, had Harold advanced his whole army, he would have swept the Normans off the field in confusion, many being caught up by the boggy streams. It may even be the case that this was an organized counter-attack, since only Wace relates that Harold ordered his men to stand firm throughout the forthcoming battle. The scene in the Tapestry that portrays the death of his brothers Gyrth and Leofwine comes immediately before the scene of the Norman cavalry falling by the hillock, which could suggest that they led such an attack. If it were an organized counter it was launched too early, before the Normans had weakened sufficiently, but would be in keeping with Harold's impetuous nature.

At this juncture, there must have been a pause in the battle. The Normans had need to reform their shaken troops, the English to assess the damage to their right wing and send men to reinforce it as necessary. The opportunity would have been taken by Harold to allow whatever food and water was available to be passed to his men. Similarly the Normans would have been resting after their exertions and horses would be watered in the streams on the valley floor. William must have been inwardly worried by the course of the battle. It was now early afternoon and the English still held the ridge. If Harold could hold out until evening the Normans would have to withdraw. They would have been tired, low in morale, unable to forage in areas not yet devastated because of the close proximity of the English army, their retreat to Normandy cut off by a fleet. William could not even afford to draw the battle.

## The Feigned Flights

Once again the foot-soldiers and cavalry came up the slopes and the bitter fighting resumed, but still the Normans could not break the line. Whenever a group of knights broke in they were thrown out by weight of numbers; nor could they outflank their opponents because of the steeper slopes and thick vegetation. The only way to disorganize the English line was to lure them out and it is not unreasonable to credit the Duke himself with this ruse. Poitiers explains that, remembering how the Breton flight had encouraged their enemies to break ranks, William organized deliberate, feigned flights to achieve the same end. Numbers of knights would suddenly jerk their horses round

◀ *Bishop Odo is prominently displayed as he rallies horsemen who have panicked at the Breton débâcle. The word 'Pueros' (young men who are not yet knights) which captions the incident is a restoration and has been questioned. Odo may be wearing a padded garment instead of his mail. It has been suggested that this is a 'Jazerant'(a light coat lined with some stout material), but that garment probably did not arrive from the east until the time of the crusades of the 12th century. He carries a 'baculum', a baton of command which distinguished its bearer from those using maces. Odo probably did not participate in the actual fighting.*

and gallop back so that the English were drawn out in the heat of battle and ran downhill in pursuit. This fatal mistake allowed the Normans to halt, wheel about and gallop back through their enemies. Poitiers asserts that such a ruse was twice used successfully, presumably in different parts of the field.

The feigned flight has long been the centre of argument. Opponents maintain that it was simply a way for the chroniclers to cover up the fact that their own horsemen ran away, but being able to outstrip their pursuers were able to recover. However, the earlier retreat was not concealed. It is also stated that such a manoeuvre would have been liable to panic the rest of the army into a real flight and that the word could not be passed to numerous horsemen without the enemy guessing what was happening. Yet there would have been many occasions when squadrons were grouping on the valley floor to recover breath while comrades fought on the hilltop, presenting opportunities for the strategy to be agreed. The fact that a number of knights fought in a *conroi* made up of men trained together in arms over the years meant that they were supremely capable of enacting a concerted manoeuvre when necessary. They needed only to wheel and follow the gonfanon of their lord as he led them in the pre-arranged feigned flight. Thus there would be no need to involve large numbers in the exercise, though this may have been done simply by instructing several *conrois* to act in unison. Such flights are well testified in warfare; Normans used them near Arques in 1052-3 and at Cassel in 1071 as well as at Messina in Sicily in 1060.

It is worth noting that, while the chroniclers agree that feigned flights took place, they do not all place them in a similar juxtaposition to other events in the battle. It has been suggested that the Tapestry shows Odo encouraging the young men during the feigned flight rather than the actual flight of the Bretons and that the disaster at the hillock formed part of this episode, an arrangement supported by the account of William of Malmesbury who used the Tapestry when writing his *Gesta Regum*; Henry of Huntingdon has a similar story. This would then put the rout of the Bretons after the feigned flight. However, William of Poitiers, who knew men who fought at Hastings, makes a point of saying that the real flight gave rise to the idea for a feigned flight. In addition, the hillock and streams of the Asten Brook on the west of the field ideally fit a picture of knights riding over it into the bogs beyond, and this seems to be where the Bretons were stationed in the battle. Since Poitiers points out that they really fled, it seems hardly likely that this would be repeated as a feigned flight at the same place. Wace follows Poitiers in seeing a disaster during the retreat of the Bretons, but places this after the feigned flight, as does the *Carmen*.

As the autumn afternoon wore on the English still held the ridge. William knew that his position was becoming serious, for there was little time left before the sun set. Whenever English fyrdmen had left their position to pursue the Norman cavalry they had been cut down by wheeling knights; the numbers on the ridge had been thinned (Malmesbury considered the success of the feigned flight as the turning-point of the battle). Many housecarls and thegns had died, their places taken by the less well-armed fyrd behind who posed less of a threat to the Normans; yet at no time had the invaders got a firm foothold on the hilltop. The position was made worse by the numbers of dead men and horses now sprawled in front of the English line, producing an additional obstacle. The knights had been in the saddle for most of the day, their horses were blown. Many had lost their mounts and were now forced to fight on foot. William himself, Poitiers assures us, had three horses killed under him that day.

Wace, who perhaps received much oral tradi-

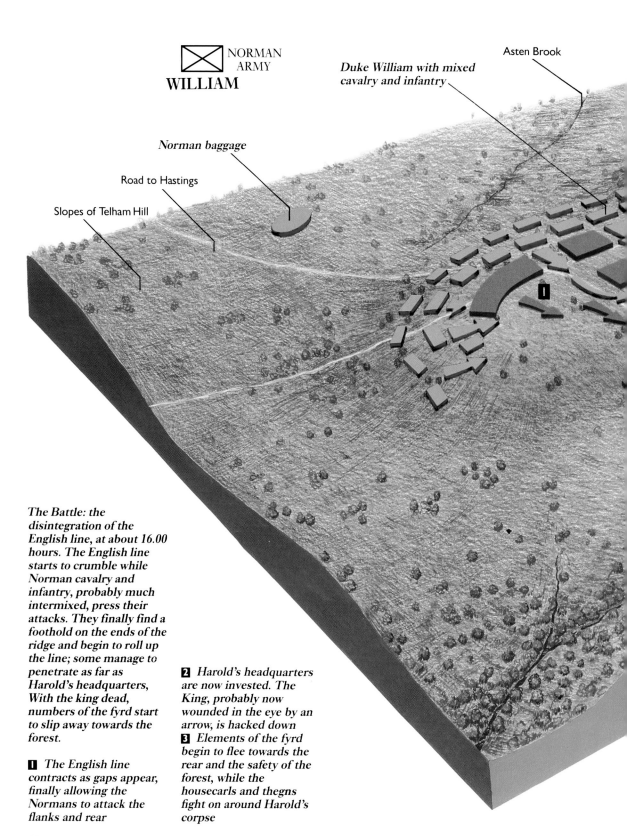

NORMAN
ARMY
**WILLIAM**

*Duke William with mixed cavalry and infantry*

Asten Brook

Norman baggage

Road to Hastings

Slopes of Telham Hill

The Battle: the disintegration of the English line, at about 16.00 hours. The English line starts to crumble while Norman cavalry and infantry, probably much intermixed, press their attacks. They finally find a foothold on the ends of the ridge and begin to roll up the line; some manage to penetrate as far as Harold's headquarters. With the king dead, numbers of the fyrd start to slip away towards the forest.

**1** The English line contracts as gaps appear, finally allowing the Normans to attack the flanks and rear

**2** Harold's headquarters are now invested. The King, probably now wounded in the eye by an arrow, is hacked down
**3** Elements of the fyrd begin to flee towards the rear and the safety of the forest, while the housecarls and thegns fight on around Harold's corpse

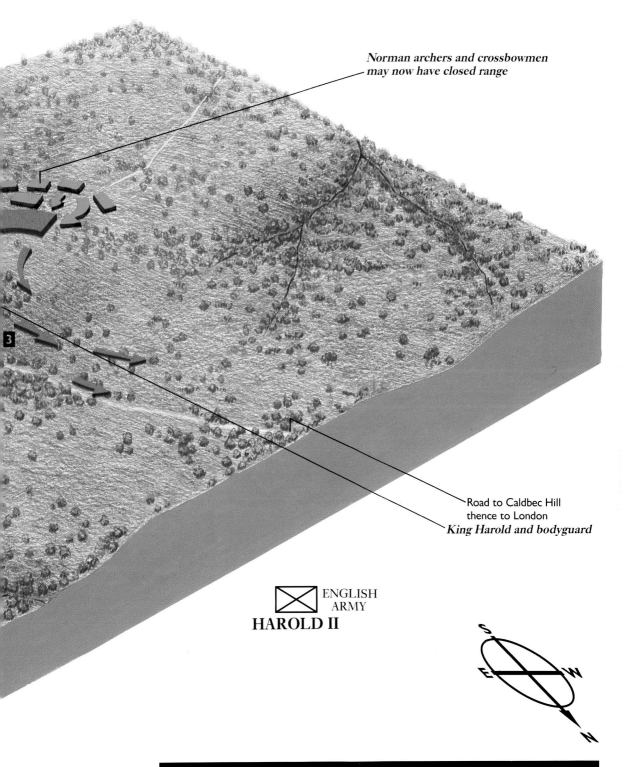

*Norman archers and crossbowmen
may now have closed range*

Road to Caldbec Hill
thence to London
*King Harold and bodyguard*

ENGLISH
ARMY
**HAROLD II**

# THE BATTLE OF HASTINGS

**The final Norman assault and the death of King Harold, about 4 p.m., 14 October 1066, as seen from the north**

*◄Many Englishmen are depicted wielding the axe from the left shoulder to take an oncoming opponent on the unshielded right side, but this could also be an accident of design. Since the two-handed grip prevented a man from using his shield, warriors may have been trained to fight in groups whereby an axeman was guarded by the shield of a companion armed with spear or sword. The early 12th-century Gesta Herewardi speaks of spearmen in Flanders carrying javelins and being protected by an axeman with a shield.*

tion and who must be used with care, none the less provides the most stirring stories; how Robert fitzErneis rode for the English standard, killing one man with his sword before being cut down with axes as he tried to beat it down; how the men of Kent and Essex fought so well; how a wrestler ducked the Duke's blow and dented William's helmet with his axe before retiring to the ranks, only to be killed by the lances of William's bodyguard.

### The Final Assault

The Duke used all his soldiers in a last concerted effort to break the enemy line. The archers began to assail the English with arrows. Presumably fresh supplies had arrived, and the Tapestry, almost as if by emphasis, shows large quivers standing next to the small figures that now form a continuous line in the lower margins. There is no reference in contemporary chronicles to the archers shooting a high trajectory cloud of arrows to fall on the

heads of the English and on the less protected fyrd in the rear ranks. It first finds mention in Henry of Huntingdon and is then expanded upon by Wace. The Tapestry gives no real hint but does suggest the importance of the archers at this stage of the battle by the sheer number shown. It could be said that a few of the archers are depicted with somewhat elevated bows but not noticeably more so than at the start of the battle. The archers may have sent in a short barrage that no doubt would have had more effect on the mauled English line than it had had previously. The infantry and knights would then have advanced until the English drew back and the archers once more loosed their arrows. It is also possible, however, that because the elements of the Norman army were now intermixed after hours of combat and that many groups were fighting at the ridge rather than cooperating in well-organized lines, the archers were forced to aim high to avoid hitting their own men. Their shafts would then have fallen on the rear ranks of the English.

HARO LD:REX: INTERFEC TVS:EST

*▲ The death of Harold. Several years ago it was suggested that the same figure never appeared twice in the same scene and that the left-hand figure was not Harold. The king was the falling warrior above whom the inscription ends; a misreading in the early 12th century by Baudri of Bourgeuil then started the arrow-in-the-eye story. It*

*is now considered that both probably represent the king, first hit in or above the eye by an arrow and later cut down. The sword is shown by the thigh of the falling figure, for which stroke, says William of Malmesbury, the knight was dismissed the army. The windsock dragon banner can be seen on the left.*

### The Death of Harold

It was at this time that King Harold was killed. Unfortunately Poitiers is very uninformative in his dealings with the subject, confining himself to a brief statement without giving any details. The Tapestry's depiction has itself come in for a great deal of interpretation over the years. It portrays a profiled figure holding an arrow that seems to have struck him either in or above the eye. To his right a second figure falls, the sword of a mounted knight close to his thigh. Above the whole group is the latin legend: 'Here King Harold has been killed'. It is now believed that Harold is first depicted as struck by an arrow and later cut down as mounted knights finally break into the defended headquarters where the royal banner flies. The reticence of Poitiers may stem from the fact that Harold's death was rather inglorious since Malmesbury, whose account follows the Tapestry, says that the arrow penetrated the brain and that, as the King lay prostrate, a knight gashed his thigh with a sword. For this act he was stripped of his knighthood and banished from the army by the Duke. Wace elaborates as usual; the King is struck above the right eye and tries to pull the arrow out, but the shaft breaks in his hand; he is then hacked down. The *Carmen* gives an account of William himself bursting through the ranks of housecarls with three named knights and hacking down the

King but such a deed would have been well chronicled by every French writer and ballad singer, which it is not. One recent theory for the omission of evidence for an arrow wound in the early chronicles is that the incident as shown on the Tapestry was a symbolic representation of blinding as a divine punishment, an artistic portrayal of God's displeasure that may be detected in various parts of the Tapestry. This latter idea brings us back to the notion that the arrow-in-the-eye story began with a misreading of the Tapestry but it seems likely that near-contemporaries would have understood the meaning of a medieval embroidery and that such a well-known story would not have found such widespread favour so soon after the event had it been inaccurate.

## The Norman Victory

With the death of Harold the resistance of the English began to crumble. The red dragon windsock banner was beaten down and the royal banner of the Fighting Man seized and carried off, later to be sent to the pope in thanks for the gift of his own banner to William. The death of the King no doubt precipitated the flight of a number of fyrdmen who began to slip away along the neck of land in rear towards the safety of the forest. This together with losses from wounds, had caused the line to contract just enough for the Normans to force themselves on to the crest of the ridge probably initially at the western end. At last they were able to attack the flanks of the English position and slowly roll up the line. Though lesser fyrdmen might leave the field, the royal hearth troops, the housecarls and king's thegns, gathered around the body of Harold and sold their lives dearly.

Many Englishmen were now making a bid to escape the field. The horses tethered in rear were seized, no doubt with scant regard to the rightful owners. The thick forest that loomed beyond Caldbec Hill in the gathering gloom of the late afternoon offered potential safety especially from the horsemen, who were unsure of the ground. Wounded men hauled themselves into the woods and died there; others were found lying by the trackways.

▶ *A Norman archer. Most were unarmoured, only one mailed man being visible on the Bayeux Tapestry. He carries a self-bow almost as tall as himself but draws only to the jaw or chest. Because of the archer's long-distance role and the expense of swords, it is unlikely that many carried much more than a knife for protection. (Rick Scollins)*

◀ *The spot where Harold fell defending his banners is marked by a commemoration stone where the high altar of the 11th century church is thought to have been.*

## The Malfosse Incident

There remains to be mentioned the incident at the 'Malfosse' or 'Evil Ditch'. According to Poitiers, during the pursuit north of the battlefield Norman knights encountered a number of Englishmen who made a stand close by an old rampart or entrenchment (possibly man-made) additionally protected by a number of ditches. These may have been survivors of the battle, or perhaps latecomers only just arrived and spoiling for a fight. The Normans were taken aback and when the Duke arrived, the stump of a broken lance in his hand, he found Eustace of Boulogne with a contingent of 50 knights about to retreat. While William remonstrated, a blow struck Eustace between the shoulder blades with such force that the blood poured from his nose and mouth and he was carried away badly wounded. Notwithstanding, the Duke led his men on and mopped up this last pocket of resistance.

A different story is told by nearly all the chroniclers. Some versions appear to occur during the battle, and it is extremely likely that these in fact refer to the incident at the hillock and marshy ground previously described. Others vary the type of obstacle encountered. Orderic Vitalis, in his interpolations of William of Jumièges (before 1109 to after 1113), describes an ancient rampart hidden by long grass, at which the riders fall. In his own *Ecclesiastical History* (the relevant section finished about 1120) Orderic seems to combine Poitiers' account with his own, so that the Normans ride into the rampart and, seeing this as well as an entrenchment and many ditches, a number of Englishmen make a stand. Orderic mentions one casualty as being Engenulf, Castellan of Laigle, and it may be that he received the story from that family. It is not until the *Battle Abbey Chronicle* of c.1180 that the deep pit, as it now becomes, is given the name of 'Malfosse'. Unfortunately Wace, the great storyteller, makes no mention of the incident, which may be significant. Possibly there were two incidents, one at the hillock and streams during the battle, a second during the pursuit. It is worrying that no chronicler mentions both; perhaps garbled versions were picked up and latched on to one version or the other. If only one occurred, it was almost certainl the incident during the battle, since the Malfosse has never been satisfactorily located but the hilloc can still be seen. Moreover the Malfosse inciden seems to show much less continuity of description.

The sun set that evening at 17.04, leaving littl time for a thorough pursuit. The comment in th Interpolations of Jumièges that the Norman chased Englishmen until the following morning i a wild exaggeration. Modern experiments hav shown that by 18.15 hours the area would hav become so dark and the ground so treacherous a to make mounted pursuit impossible. The moon which was low that night, did not appear unti midnight. As the light faded William rode back t the field to survey the scene. Poitiers recalls ho the Duke was moved to pity to see so man Englishmen lying dead on the hilltop. The bodie of Gyrth and Leofwine were found near Harold The 12th century *De Inventione S. Crucis* o Waltham Abbey carries the story that the King body at first could not be identified, possibl because the arrow wound had caused too great disfigurement or because of subsequent mutil ation. In order to find the King, they sent for Edit Swan-Neck, Harold's wife 'in the Danish man ner', who knew marks on his body that only sh would have recognized. Edith, who tradition re lates was waiting by the Watch Oak on the south western slopes of Caldbec Hill, was brought to th blood-stained field and carried out her last duty t her lover. She found Harold's body among th heaps of the dead.

The royal corpse was carried to William camp and there handed over to the half-Englis knight William Malet for burial. Harold's mothe Gytha, offered its weight in gold but the Duk refused to release it to her, considering it unseeml to receive such a gift. Moreover he felt that Harol should not be buried as his mother wished whe so many lay uninterred because of his avarice. Th Normans said in jest that Harold should be burie so that he could continue to guard the shore h had tried so hard to defend. It is noteworthy th already in Malmesbury's account there appears th story that William, refusing payment, allowe Gytha to bury the body at Harold's church o Waltham Holy Cross in Essex. Wace agrees b

THIS STONE MARKS THE POSITION
OF THE HIGH ALTAR
BEHIND WHICH KING HAROLD
IS SAID TO HAVE FALLEN AT THE
1066

*A modern plaque by the foundations of the early church at Waltham Abbey in Essex records the supposed grave of Harold. Although William at first refused the body Christian burial, it seems likely that it was finally brought to Harold's church here. The tomb originally lay within the church but the east end was demolished during the 16th-century Reformation, leaving the nave to form a parish church.*

mentions no names; in his time Waltham was a royal abbey under Henry II's patronage. Inevitably tories arose that the King had escaped from the battle, having further adventures until he died a hermit at Chester.

On Sunday 15 October the day was given over to burial of the Norman dead. Those English men or women who came to the field were permitted to take friends or relatives away, but many were left on the ridge in the same way as at Stamford Bridge, where Orderic reported seeing piles of bones some 70 years after the battle. The chronicler Jumièges mentions that loot was taken at the field of Hastings and the Bayeux Tapestry shows that this had already begun during the battle; the lower borders, though somewhat restored, illus-

trate figures stripping the dead of their mail. The Duke may have given orders for the construction on Caldbec Hill of a Mountjoy, or victory cairn of stones, since the area still bears the name.

Shortly after, William returned to the camp at Hastings. Here he waited five days, partly to rest his weary troops and partly to await the arrival of a deputation from the English leaders. When none came, he marched from the camp with his remaining forces, no doubt leaving a strong garrison behind. The numbers of men must have been severely thinned after the battle, perhaps by 25 to 30 per cent, and by the end of October much needed reinforcements had arrived from across the Channel. William's route can be tentatively reconstructed from chroniclers' reports and the areas of waste recorded in Domesday Book. He moved towards Dover, detaching troops en route to punish the town of Old Romney whose inhabitants had killed either the crew of two stray invasion ships or a foraging party. Dover submitted and William placed a castle within the fortress on the cliffs. Squires fired several houses but William made reparation for them. While here the army

# William's March to London, October to December 1(

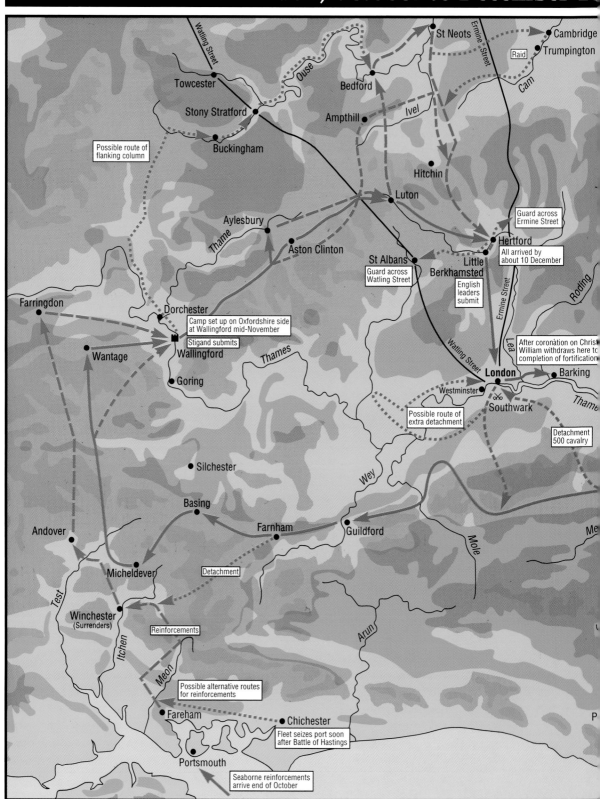

Watling Street

Towcester

Stony Stratford

Buckingham

**Possible route of flanking column**

Ouse

St Neots

Bedford

Ampthill

Ivel

Hitchin

Luton

Cambridge

Trumpington

**Raid**

Cam

Ermine Street

Aylesbury

Thame

Aston Clinton

St Albans

**Guard across Watling Street**

Little Berkhamsted

**English leaders submit**

Hertford

**Guard across Ermine Street**

**All arrived by about 10 December**

Ermine Street

Roding

Farringdon

Dorchester

**Camp set up on Oxfordshire side at Wallingford mid-November**

**Stigand submits**

Wantage

Wallingford

Goring

Thames

Watling Street

Lea

**After coronation on Christ... William withdraws here to completion of fortification**

London

Barking

Westminster

Thame

Southwark

**Possible route of extra detachment**

**Detachment 500 cavalry**

Silchester

Wey

Mole

Me

Basing

Andover

Farnham

Guildford

**Detachment**

Micheldever

Test

Winchester

**(Surrenders)**

**Reinforcements**

Itchen

Meon

**Possible alternative routes for reinforcements**

Arun

Fareham

Chichester

**Fleet seizes port soon after Battle of Hastings**

Portsmouth

**Seaborne reinforcements arrive end of October**

P

was stricken with dysentery, but, leaving the sick behind, the Duke proceeded to Canterbury where representatives came out to submit before he reached the city. The men of Kent also now yielded. William himself was taken ill but determined to press on as forage was needed for the army.

In London there was panic as the Normans approached. Either or both Stigand of Canterbury and Ealdred of York elected the young Edgar Atheling as king, probably supported by Earls Edwin and Morcar. There seemed no set plan of resistance, however. Wary of the power of the city of London, William veered westwards. A large detachment advanced to the city where it fired Southwark after skirmishing with Londoners who had crossed London Bridge. William may have hoped to seize the city by surprise, or it may have been a diversionary tactic to allow the main army to pass by to the south. The detachment rejoined the main force that continued into Hampshire and Berkshire, dividing into columns that wasted the countryside partly for food and partly to intimidate London. Winchester's submission now meant that the capital of Wessex as well as the episcopal capital and the south-east ports were under William's control. He crossed the Thames at Wallingford where Archbishop Stigand came to submit and dissociate himself from Edgar. Having placed a castle in the Anglo-Saxon burh William now moved north and east, finally turning south to (probably Little) Berkhamsted in Hertfordshire. Here he was met by Ealdred, Edgar and several magnates who possibly included Edwin and Morcar. The latter earls, having declined to fight at Hastings, according to Malmesbury, now tried to make one or the other of themselves king and when that failed disappeared northwards, hoping

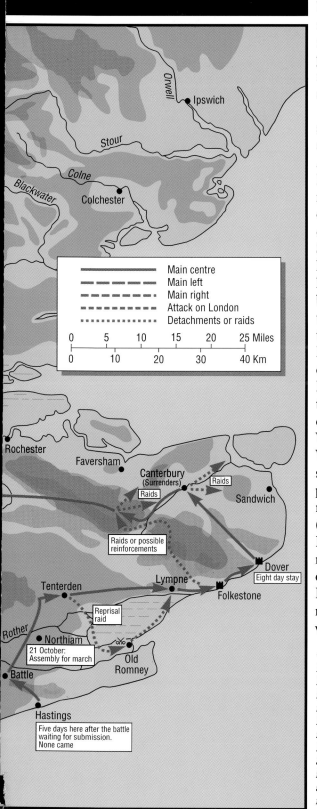

◀ *William's march to London, October–December 1066. This map is based on areas of waste recorded in Domesday Book and the conclusions reached by Baring, Lemmon and Beeler. Slight variations on the illustrated route can be argued; for example reinforcements may have* *landed at Chichester, Portsmouth or Fareham. The exact dates of each march are based partly on calculation. The direction was determined by the huge woodland areas and the Roman roads, as well as by William's desire to seize important towns and intimidate London into submission.*

◀ *Dover castle originated as an Iron Age fortress which became an Anglo-Saxon fortified 'burh'. The late 10th or early 11th-century church of St. Mary-in-Castro utilized the Roman 'Pharos' or lighthouse as a bell-tower. A Norman ditch and bank were discovered near the south transept of the church and the Conqueror's defences may have consisted of a simple enclosure, The later expansion north with its stone fortifications appears to have been begun during the 12th century by Henry II. (Cambridge University Collection; copyright reserved).*

that safety lay in Northumbria. If so, they may have submitted at Barking after the coronation.

William is supposed to have been wary of immediately accepting the crown because of the numerous rebels still to be dealt with. He was persuaded by the army and also by the English delegation who wished to have a king and who pointed out that as king he would be more able to suppress further revolt. William came down to London and appears to have entered without incident, though Jumièges tells of a skirmish at the gates and the *Carmen* describes elaborate siege works and negotiations. The march from Hastings had covered more than 350 miles.

William was crowned in Edward the Confessor's new church at Westminster on Christmas Day, 1066. At the shout of acclamation the Norman soldiers stationed outside thought a riot had started and began firing the nearby houses. As fighting broke out many of those in the church rushed outside while William, it was reported, trembled like an aspen leaf. Having come so far and achieved so much, even at the very time of coronation it seemed that his wishes might be thwarted. Given the panic and the flames, it must have appeared that God had declared him unfit for the sacred office. In the half-empty interior, Archbishop Ealdred placed the crown of England on William's head.

▶ *In London the Conqueror sets a castle, consisting of ditch and palisades, in the south-east corner of the city on the site of the Tower of London. Bounded thus on the south and east the ditch formed a right angle to protect the northern and western sides from attack by the populace. The latter ditch is seen here as it runs down towards the river. William resided at Barking while work on a fortification – presumably this one – was in progress.*

# AFTERMATH

It cannot be said that the battle of Hastings was the final act of the Conquest. It was most certainly a decisive victory, because the King and two of his brothers, as well as many of the English aristocracy, were now slain. The slaughter of men at Fulford and Stamford Bridge not only assisted William by reducing Harold's immediate potential, but helped neutralize a serious concerted threat from the north. In addition, the lack of castles in England before the Conquest was seen as a reason for the ease of William's takeover. There were no fortified pockets from which armed men could harry his forces and supply lines during a march. By contrast, William threw up castles everywhere. However, it would be perhaps three more years before he could feel secure in his new kingdom.

The first revolts manifested themselves shortly after his coronation. Having returned to Normandy in March 1067, William left Bishop Odo and his seneschal, William fitzOsbern, in charge but their methods were heavy handed. In the west Edric the Wild devastated Herefordshire; in the east the men of Kent invited Eustace of Boulogne to attack Dover, a move beaten off by the Norman garrison. Overseas, English dissidents were stirring up trouble, notably at the court of King Swein of Denmark. The latter had a claim to the English throne that seemed more attractive now that Hardrada of Norway was dead.

William returned to spend Christmas in London and early in 1068 marched on Exeter, which submitted and was given a castle. The castellan

▲The White Tower, the central keep in the Tower of London, begun for the Conqueror by Bishop Gundulph of Rochester in about 1078 and completed in about 1100. In front, the late 12th-century fragment of the Wardrobe Tower is sited on the line of the Roman eastern city wall which can be traced on the grass. Thus the first Norman castle here was set in a corner of the Roman defences and was cut off from the city by a ditch and palisade.

▶William's later campaigns, 1067-72. William's marches are reconstructed from the chronicler's accounts of his movements and the Roman road network. On his second march northward in the spring of 1069, the route to and from York was probably via Ermine Street, passing Lincoln and Tadcaster. Winchester has also been suggested as a starting-point for each campaign.

# William's Later Campaigns, 1067-1072

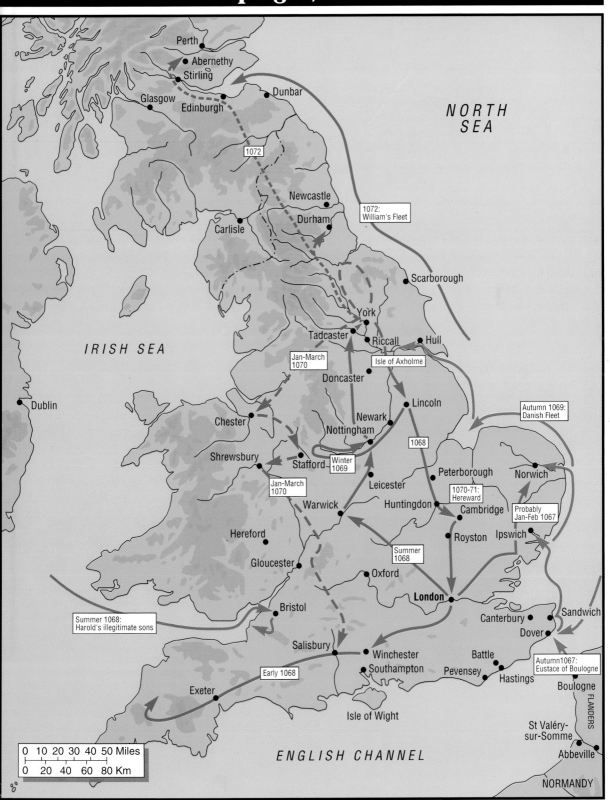

NORTH SEA

Perth
Abernethy
Stirling
Glasgow
Edinburgh
Dunbar

1072

Newcastle
Carlisle
Durham

1072:
William's Fleet

Scarborough

IRISH SEA

York
Tadcaster
Riccall    Hull
Isle of Axholme

Jan-March
1070

Doncaster

Dublin

Lincoln

Autumn 1069:
Danish Fleet

Chester
Newark
Nottingham

1068

Shrewsbury
Stafford    Winter
1069

Peterborough
Norwich

Jan-March
1070

Leicester

1070-71:
Hereward

Warwick

Huntingdon
Cambridge

Probably
Jan-Feb 1067

Hereford

Royston    Ipswich

Summer
1068

Gloucester
Oxford

London

Summer 1068:
Harold's illegitimate sons

Bristol

Canterbury
Sandwich

Dover

Salisbury
Winchester
Battle

Early 1068
Southampton
Pevensey
Hastings

Boulogne

Autumn1067:
Eustace of Boulogne

FLANDERS

Exeter

St Valéry-
sur-Somme

Isle of Wight

St Valéry-
sur-Somme

ENGLISH CHANNEL

Abbeville

0 10 20 30 40 50 Miles
0 20 40 60 80 Km

NORMANDY

later pushed into Cornwall to establish Norman rule. In the summer three illegitimate sons of Harold landed from Ireland but were beaten off by the men of Somerset. When revolt broke out in Devon and Cornwall the following year the men of Exeter, mindful of the royal power, dealt with the trouble.

William's wife, Mathilda, came over in the spring of 1068, to be crowned at Westminster. At about this time Edgar removed himself to Scotland while Edwin and Morcar began to foment trouble; Edwin was said to have been denied the promise of William's daughter in marriage. The northern earls allied with their nephew, Bleddyn of Wales, and a northern insurrection seemed likely. William marched to meet it, planting castles as he went. While one was being erected at Warwick, Edwin and Morcar submitted; while work was starting on the castle of Nottingham, York surrendered. Malcolm of Scotland made peace with the King's representative, the Bishop of Durham. William then built a motte in York itself before returning south, placing castles at Lincoln, Huntingdon and Cambridge.

The following year the north again caused trouble. In January Robert of Commines, the first Norman Earl of Northumbria, was killed at Durham. As unrest spread the constable of York castle was also slain. Edgar appeared from Scotland with Cospatric and other Northumbrians, marched on York and attacked both city and castle. William Malet sent word that he could not hold out much longer in York and William came rapidly north in a march that can be compared with Harold's in 1066. Edgar was forced back to Scotland and a second castle was planted on the other bank of the Ouse. William returned south but a Danish fleet soon appeared off the east coast. Estimated at between 240 and 300 ships, the fleet included three of King Swein's sons and a brother. It plundered its way north via Dover, Sandwich, Ipswich and Norfolk and sailed into the Humber. Edgar once more appeared, as did Earls Cospatric, Waltheof and others. As the invaders approached York, William Malet fired the houses near the castle to prevent them being used but the flames spread even to the Minster. The garrison made a sortie which was defeated and the city was pillaged. King William came north, leaving his subordinate commanders to deal with additional

▶ *The keep or 'donjon' of Chepstow castle in Gwent is one of the earliest such structures in England. It was built by William fitzOsbern, Seneschal of Normandy and close friend of the Conqueror, created Earl of Hereford soon after the Conquest. The lower part of the keep, together with sections of the stone curtain wall on the southern side, survive from the work of 1067-72.*

◀ *Clifford's Tower in York, probably the motte that was erected in 1068 as part of the earth and timber castle to house a garrison and watch the city. The stonework on the summit is 13th century in date. A second motte across the river, the Old Baile, may be that built the following year in response to further unrest.*

revolts in Devon and Cornwall, Dorset and Somerset, and Cheshire. The Danes retreated before him down the Humber to the Isle of Axholme and then to Yorkshire again. Leaving his half-brother, Robert of Mortain, to watch them he crossed the Pennines to suppress a revolt in Staffordshire, then came back to Nottingham and thence finally to York where the Danes withdrew and were bought off. The King celebrated Christmas in the city before devastating the area. The 'harrying of the north' was a brutal act that not only

affected Yorkshire but also tracts of Cheshire, Shropshire, Staffordshire and Derbyshire.

In the New Year William moved to the Tees where Waltheof and Cospatric submitted, then marched back to York through difficult terrain in bitter winter weather before setting off over the Pennines with equally harsh weather, bad terrain and mutinous mercenaries, to relieve Shrewsbury and pacify Cheshire. Chester and Stafford castles were planted and the King finally came south to Salisbury and paid off his troops (except the mutineers, who had to stay another forty days).

Thus by the spring of 1070 William had effectively broken the worst of the opposition to his position. Between 1070 and 1071 he faced a gathering in the East Anglian fens which included Danes together with Earl Morcar (Edwin being dead) and Hereward the Wake; a causeway driven into the fens broke their resistance. In fact unrest in Maine and Flanders at the same time caused more concern than these last pockets of revolt in England. The devastated north now offered a potential prize to the Scottish king, however, so in 1072 an expedition by land and sea northwards persuaded Malcolm to become William's vassal, and Edgar Aetheling was expelled from the Scottish court. Henceforth opposition to the King would come from his sons, his magnates and his neighbours across the Channel.

The Normans took over many fine Anglo-Saxon institutions: the government, the royal seal, the king's writ, the many mints producing coins of quality. The lands of those natives who had died or fled were given predominantly to Normans or their allies, especially Bretons and Flemings. They stepped into many positions in the Church, built castles and impressive stone cathedrals. The English were seen as the underdogs yet the language survived because of the sheer numbers who continued to speak it. Norman efficiency was absorbed into the culture, a new dynasty sat on the throne and England was forced to look to the continent rather than towards Scandinavia. William died in 1087 from internal rupture sustained while engaged in quelling revolt at Mantes in the Vexin on the Norman border. His grandchildren saw Normandy gradually separate from England, as a native Anglo-Norman race developed.

▼ *The Conqueror was buried in the Abbaye aux Hommes at Caen, one of two founded by the Duke and Duchess in the town, the other being the Abbaye aux Dames wherein is buried his wife Mathilda. The* *Conqueror's grave was destroyed by Calvinists in the 16th century. Recently a single thighbone was discovered that indicated a man some five feet eight inches tall. (Courtesy of the French Government Tourist Office)*

# THE BATTLEFIELD TODAY

The town of Battle is situated seven miles north of Hastings on the modern A2100 road from London to the coast. There is a small museum, but hardly any relics of the battle survive. The High Street runs along the eastern side of the neck of land leading to the ridge, much of the latter being obscured by the buildings of the later abbey. Entry to the abbey grounds is via the car park, slightly west of the 14th-century gatehouse, which stands to one side of a square at the bottom of the High Street.

Some areas of the ridge have been altered since 1066. The Conqueror ordered the monks to place the abbey at the top of the slope with the high altar on the spot where Harold fell, rather than in the valley, which was more level and was fed by streams. Thus part of the ground at the top of the slope has been altered from its original state, while nearly all the buildings are post-Norman in date. The dormitory, which runs down the slope, is built on stepped undercrofts. To the east a building platform was erected, the reredorter placed along the hillside and the ground inside and behind on the northern side levelled. Subsequently this was even more built up. The open courtyard leading from the gatehouse was built up and levelled during the 16th century, burying the windows of the cellerer's undercroft, which survives on the slope at the west of the monastery.

The slope of the hill was thus steeper in 1066 than it now appears. Today the western end has a gradient of one in 33, that near the road one in fifteen. The flanks are one in twelve and the rear one in four. At the highest part of the ridge, to the north of the monastic buildings, the foundations of the east end of the original Norman church were located only a few inches below the modern topsoil of the floor of the later church. Three stone crypt chapels of the latter can be seen. The high altar commemorated the place of Harold's fall and the position is now marked by a modern memorial stone set in the earth. A second, smaller marker a few feet away gives a more recent estimate of the position. Perhaps the most original part of the ridge lies near Pyke House, for the English line ran beyond the abbey buildings to east and west. At the western end, looking down from the cellerer's undercroft, the hillock can be seen to the right. Beyond it the boggy stream was dammed to form a series of fish-ponds for the abbey. Telham Hill rises in the distance and can be reached by continuing out along the modern A2100 road, which partly follows the old road. This crosses the saddle between the streams roughly between the Lodge of Battle Abbey Park and the railway station. Farther along the road south, the track to Telham Court leads to the point on the old road from which the English position would have become visible (this view is now obscured by trees). Just over a mile beyond, the modern road crosses Blackhorse Hill, where William probably halted to arm.

Returning towards the town, a left turn into Powdermill Lane passes behind the Norman lines and affords a view of the ridge. Continuing back into the High Street, Whatlington Road is a turning on the right at the northern end; approximately 500 yards along it a pathway leads to the white windmill, which marks Caldbec Hill.

On the battlefield itself, the English line ran along approximately below the cellerer's undercroft eastwards through the dormitory building to end about 50 yards south of the Primary School. It probably ran west for approximately 150 yards beyond Princess Elizabeth's Lodgings. The French and Flemish division may have rested their left near the Lodge of the Park, while the Norman division may have stretched from here to a position level with the twin towers of the Princess Elizabeth's Lodgings by the cellerer's undercroft.

# CHRONOLOGY

## Events leading up to the Campaign of 1066

**1035:** Death of King Cnut. Succeeded by his son, Harold I.

**1036:** Blinding and death of Edward's brother Alfred on return from exile.

**1040:** Harthacnut succeeds his half-brother Harold I.

**1042:** Edward the Confessor returns from exile to become king of England.

**1047:** William defeats Norman rebels at Val-ès-Dunes.

**1051:** Revolt of Earl Godwin and his sons, who are banished. William promised the crown; possible visit of William to England.

**1052:** Godwin returns; many Norman favourites expelled.

**1054:** William defeats French/Angevin force at Mortemer.

**1055:** Revolt of Aelfgar of Mercia and Gruffydd of Wales; settlement reached.

**1057:** William defeats rearguard of second French/Angevin invasion force at Varaville.

**1060:** Death of King Henry of France and Count Geoffrey of Anjou.

**1062:** Second revolt of Aelfgar and Gruffydd. Death of Aelfgar. His son, Edwin, succeeds him in Mercia. Midwinter campaign against Gruffydd by Harold.

**1063:** Death of Gruffydd after two-pronged attack by Harold and Tostig. Normans occupy Maine.

**1064** or possibly **1065:** Harold travels to Normandy. Expedition to Brittany; oath to William before returning to England.

**1065:** Tostig expelled from Northumbria and Edwin's brother, Morcar, installed.

**5 January 1066:** Edward dies.

**6 January 1066:** Edward is buried; coronation of Harold.

## The Campaign of 1066

**May:** Tostig attacks the east coast of England. Rebuffed, he sails to Scotland.

**September:** Tostig and Harald Hardrada sail into the Humber.

**8 September:** Harold disbands his army.

**12 September:** William moves his fleet to St. Valéry-sur-Somme.

**20 September:** Battle of Gate Fulford. Edwin and Morcar defeated by Hardrada and Tostig; York surrenders.

**20-24 September:** Harold marches north.

**25 September:** Battle of Stamford Bridge. English defeat Norwegians; Hardrada and Tostig killed.

**28 September:** William lands at Pevensey.

**1 October:** Harold informed of Norman landing and marches south.

**6-11 October:** Harold in London.

**13 October:** Harold arrives at rendezvous of Caldbec Hill.

**14 October:** Battle of Hastings. Norman victory; Harold killed, together with brothers Gyrth and Leofwine.

**25 December:** William crowned at Westminster.

## Events following the Campaign of 1066

**January-February 1067:** William at Barking; probable progress through East Anglia to Norwich.

**March 1067:** William visits Normandy; Edric ravages Herefordshire.

**Autumn 1067:** Eustace of Boulogne attacks Dover, but is beaten off. William returns at Christmas.

**Early 1068:** William marches on Exeter. Mathilda crowned queen. First visit of William to York.

**Summer 1068:** Sons of Harold from Ireland beaten off by men of Exeter.

January 1069: Robert of Commines killed and north in revolt.

February to early April 1069: Second visit of William to York.

Autumn 1069: Danish fleet appears; north again in revolt.

Winter 1070: Third visit of William to York and devastation of north. Revolts in Cheshire and Shrewsbury and West Country suppressed.

1070-71: Revolt in the Fens suppressed.

1072: Expedition to the north and submission of Malcolm of Scotland. Edgar expelled from Scottish court.

1087: Death of William I.

# A GUIDE TO FURTHER READING

Brown R. A. *The Normans and the Norman Conquest*. London, 1969. Contains a useful bibliography and background history.

– *Documents of Medieval History 5, The Norman Conquest*. London, 1984. Contains English and Norman material, the fullest treatment being given to the most contemporary.

Douglas D. *William the Conqueror*. London, 1964. A standard reference work.

Loyn, H. *Anglo-Saxon England and the Norman Conquest*. London, 1962. A more concise history than Stenton, below.

Stenton F. *The Bayeux Tapestry*. London, 2nd ed., 1965. Includes useful sections on armour and dress.

– *Anglo-Saxon England*. London, 3rd ed., 1971. Extensive coverage of the Saxon period including the Conquest, together with full bibliography.

– Whitelock, D., Douglas, D., Lemmon, C. and Barlow, F. *The Norman Conquest, its Setting and Impact*. London, 1966. Lemmon has a good account of the battle but differs in some points from others cited.

Wilson, D. *The Bayeux Tapestry*. London, 1985. Excellent colour reproduction plus text.

Various aspects of the Conquest are frequently examined in articles appearing in: *Proceedings of the Battle Abbey Conference* (1978-1981), Ipswich, 1979-1982, continued as: *Anglo-Norman Studies*, 1983 on. See especially papers by R. Abels, M. Bennett, D. J. Bernstein, C. M. Gillmor, N. Hooper, E. M. C. van Houts, J. Neumann and A. Williams.

# WARGAMING THE BATTLE OF HASTINGS

A perennial difficulty facing the wargamer wishing to re-create a particular historical battle is that both he and his players will probably know too much about it. In setting up his wargame he must take into account the way the historical protagonists fought on the day and if his players are familiar with the battle (or read it up specially in advance of the game) this inevitably influences the way they play it. The problem is particularly acute in the case of Hastings since it is, arguably, the best-known battle in English history. Even the average man (or woman) in the street will have some knowledge of the course and outcome of the battle, including the rudiments of the tactical concepts (cavalry, infantry and archers v. infantry). What then of the average wargamer? Hastings, regrettably, offers few surprises.

One common option is the 'disguised scenario'. The game designer presents his players with an anonymous version of the original battle, in which the tactical situation and balance of forces are the same although the protagonists may be different, invites them to fight it out, and only reveals the true identity at the end of the game. This is easiest to manage in periods where the weaponry and organization do not immediately identify the situation, or where there was such an abundance of actions that changing the nationality of the combatants can hide the truth. A Peninsula battle with French v. British can be translated into a Seven Years War encounter between Russian and Prussian forces, for example, with relative ease.

Hastings is a more difficult case since it is hard to find other battles where the basic tactical situation – one army based on heavy infantry and the other on cavalry, infantry and foot archers – is the same. Possibilities *do* exist, however, and might be worth looking into. The battle of Tours (AD 732) has Frankish infantry seeing off an Arab army and shares something of Hastings' pivotal historical importance. At the other end of Europe Silistria (AD 972) saw victory for a combined arms Byzantine army over the Rus shield wall, and the troop types involved are a rather closer match to the Hastings situation.

But Frankish and Rus armies are a rarity on the wargames scene, even if Arab armies are rather more familiar (if you include indeterminate 'Muslim' collections) and Byzantines are relatively common, and the trouble of finding such a matching pair is probably not worth the effort. In the end some bright spark is almost certain to note the similarity with 1066 and once spotted the disguise becomes obvious to all concerned.

Does hindsight really matter? I must confess I thought it did until I organized a re-fight of Hastings myself. As the Harold player I knew that it was absolutely essential to hold the shield wall steady and avoid a repeat of the Gyrth and Leofwine disaster. But in the excitement of mid-battle what did I do but allow one of my wings to charge downhill in pursuit of a local tactical advantage. My opponent promptly, and rightly, punished such rashness with a brisk counter-attack which proved to be the turning-point of the battle.

The lesson would seem to be, 'Never underestimate the capacity of the wargamer to lose his head in a crisis'. To create such situations you need to have a game that is close and exciting and which does not allow the player too much time to ponder his moves. To attain this desirable goal the game designer must strike a balance between the demands of the Hardware of the wargame (the playing pieces and size of table used) and its Software (the rules that regulate the course of the action) so as to achieve a reconstruction in which the two elements are in harmony, and not working against each other.

## Choice of Figures and Scale

Obtaining the hardware is the easy part, since most figure manufacturers seem honour bound to produce a 1066 range, but making a rational choice is rather more difficult. For cheapness it is hard to beat the 20mm plastic figure, and the Anglo-Saxon and Norman sets produced by Revell can be combined to make up two fine armies. The Normans are very short on cavalry, however, so you will need to exercise the art of the converter, grafting heads and torsos on to riding legs and horses from other suitable sets – in itself a rewarding activity and one which can give the wargamer the satisfaction of owning a hand-made rather than mass-produced army.

The range of available models in the traditional metal figure scales is truly vast and while it can be very effective to mix and match figures from various manufacturers care must be taken to ensure that they look right. Variations in figure size within a notional scale can be rationalized as individual differences in physique, but designers do tend to have distinctive ideas about the size of horses, in particular, so it is essential to buy sample models to check for compatibility in advance of any mass purchase.

Choice of scale is an absolutely crucial step since the size of the figures used has important consequences for the nature of the wargame that can be played with them. For many years the 25mm figure was the undisputed queen of the tabletop battlefield but while individually superior, in detail and animation, to their smaller cousins, *en masse* the 25mm figure suffers badly in comparison. It takes simply ages to paint a 25mm army, especially one containing lots of cavalry; the transportation of such an army requires both care (to avoid damage) and brute strength (because of its sheer weight!) and, finally, a battle using figures in this scale needs a rather large playing area. This is a combination that puts off many new recruits.

Fifteen-millimetre figures are available in equal, if not greater, variety and combine ease and speed of painting with relative cheapness, and a perhaps surprising degree of durability – smaller weapons and extremities being rather less vulnerable. Increasingly they are becoming the obvious choice for most pre-twentieth-century wargaming periods. Five-millimetre figures – cast individually or as blocks – also have their advantages although they are perhaps better suited to later wargaming periods than the one in question, where, assembled in large quantities they can bear a striking resemblance to contemporary prints of battles from the seventeenth century onwards. Even smaller figures *do* exist, in 2mm scale but seem to require, in this writer's opinion, something of the same suspension of disbelief as displayed in the story of the emperor's new clothes. . .

If starting from scratch, 15mm probably offers the best combination of availability, affordability, and playability, but if you are not in too much of a hurry a browse around the Bring and Buy stalls at wargaming conventions can reveal some remarkable bargains in the now unfashionable 25mm scale.

## Rules for the Wargame

Ultimately, the choice of figure scale depends largely on the sort of game you want to play. Generally speaking, the larger the figure the smaller the figure : man ratio. You can't fight a 1:1 level game with 2mm blocks! This brings us to the vexed question of Rules. In wargames terms Hastings falls within the so-called 'Ancient' period which is taken to cover anything between the early civilizations of the Middle East and the dawn of the gunpowder age. In the world of commercially available wargames rules the Ancient period is, at the time of writing (1991), in a state of considerable flux. For two decades now the field has been dominated by the rules published by the Wargames Research Group, which have been the consistent choice for both national and international wargames competitions. The virtues of the basic set – which went through six editions – were offset by challenges from players who yearned for a wargame requiring rather more generalship than gamesmanship, or from those who were looking for a more period-specific set to avoid oddities like Assyrians fighting Crusaders!

Partly in response to such criticism and partly as a result of their own theoretical development, the WRG brought out a seventh edition which was, in effect, a completely different game. Despite some manifest technical advantages, this seems not to have attained the same level of general acceptance, to the extent that competition organizers have been known to dispense with the Ancient period altogether because of players' inability to agree on which edition of the rules to use.

The situation has recently been transformed by WRG's publication of their DBA (*De Bellis Antiquitatis*) Rules, which have been designed to produce a quick, easily comprehensible wargame using small collections of figures. In this writer's opinion the WRG has done the hobby a considerable service in this set of rules which uses clever game mechanisms to produce subtle results, giving games that are quick, but usually closely fought. DBA armies, moreover, being made up of fifty figures or fewer, can be assembled and painted with remarkable speed. My own DBA Viking army was painted in a single evening! So for the player wishing to go off and wargame Hastings with the minimum of fuss, I would highly recommend the DBA system.

## Going it Alone

The historical purist, however, will feel rather cheated if his reconstruction of the battle did not require a little more effort and such a wargamer may well wish, therefore, to produce his own set of period-specific (or even battle-specific) rules. Having written many such sets of rules myself, I would agree that they can, indeed, be the best way of re-creating the tactics and atmosphere of a particular period. But is is very hard to reproduce the known tactical balance of an individual battle without so constraining the players' individual freedom of action as fatally to erode the competitive element in the reconstruction *as a wargame*. The rule-writer must beware, too, of borrowing individual mechanisms from one set of rules and trying to graft them on to another. Experience shows that the elements of a set of rules hang together as an integrated whole, and taken in isolation can produce unsatisfactory if not freakish results.

One essential factor in the Battle of Hastings, but one which is ignored in most sets of wargames rules, is that of fatigue. As long as the housecarls

can go on seeing off successive waves of Norman attacks, the English line can hold Senlac hill. But since so much of the burden of hand-to-hand combat was carried by this *minority* of the English army, the sheer physical effort of wielding their weapons began to take its toll as the battle progressed. For the Norman strike-force – the mounted knights – the physical effort was shared between man and horse and because, in addition, the Norman infantry as a whole was made up of professional mercenaries attacks could be rotated to give groups of warriors the chance of a breather. Rules, therefore, should allow for a gradual diminution in fighting effect for the housecarls as the battle progresses. Taken alongside a progressive inability to hold the full extent of the hilltop position as English losses mount up, the longer the Norman army remains in action the more the balance should tilt in its favour.

This situation is a reflection of the lack of tactical options facing the English. Basically, they had just to stand on the hilltop and endure, while the Normans could try out the full range of tactical possibilities allowed by their combined arms organization. Any Harold player thus has a pretty boring job since, unlike Wellington at Waterloo in a similar situation, his historical counterpart seems not to have had to dash back and forth dealing with crises and fine tuning the defensive line. A radical solution would be to dispense with a 'live' Harold player altogether and allow the English army to be controlled by an umpire 'auto-pilot' while the Normans operate as a multi-player team – at least three players would be ideal.

Even with such a set-up, however, the final phase of the battle, with the fall of Harold and the last stand of the housecarls, has a dramatic quality about it that deserves to be recreated in some detail on the table-top. So (if the wargame should go that way!), a fitting climax to the re-enactment might be to play through this last doomed but epic struggle as a 'skirmish' wargame on a one figure = one man ratio. For such a game the 25mm figure comes into its own, and if a suitable prize is offered, players controlling individually named Normans will find themselves competing enthusiastically for the honour of striking down the hard-fighting English king and the dragon of Wessex.